I began writing this book just after my dad died. It was a way to cope with the immensity of what had just happened. I have never had words just pour out of me before. Writing was cathartic. It uncovered parts of me that were hiding in plain sight.

I wouldn't be who I am without him.

Howard Burl Guild II was a force. He was powerful. That power didn't cease to exist simply because his soul left his body. I would argue that it became stronger. My relationship with him has changed since his death. You read that right. We still have a relationship, arguably a better one than we had near the end of his life. He lived his life remarkably well. He loved rich experiences. He moved from his heart despite being incredibly type A and a bit controlling. He was my mentor and guide and my biggest cheerleader. Every ounce of grit I have in me, I got from him. He defied the odds so many times, fighting back from the brink of death over and over again. I believe that a part of my purpose in this life was to show him what pure unconditional love could feel like. This book is in honor of his beautiful life and the impact it had on mine.

BEYOND THE TABLE

DISCOVERING THE SOUL OF SERVICE

HALEY MOORE

BELMONT, NORTH CAROLINA

Beyond the Table: Discovering the Soul of Service
Haley Moore

Copyright ©2026 Haley Moore. All rights reserved. No portion of
this book may be reproduced in any form without permission from
the author, except as permitted by United States copyright law.
Contact the author at haley@acquire-wine.com.

Published by Synergy Publishing Group, Belmont, NC
Formatting by Melisa Graham

Softcover, April 2026, ISBN 978-1-960892-66-9
Ebook, April 2026, ISBN 978-1-960892-67-6

Contents

*We are all just walking
each other home.*

—Ram Dass

Take a Seat at My Table

The table is a sacred space, a gathering place that brings people together to connect in deep and meaningful ways. It is no wonder that I dedicated so much of my life to a career in restaurants. Feeding people is the deepest way we show love. As I have moved through my life and career, the table has been a cornerstone, a place where we slow down, where we ground, where we are received in community. The table, while often literal, is also figurative. I have found tables in many forms, often including shared meals where I have been welcomed with open arms. The table is synonymous with being in community, with hospitality, with connecting deeper.

In the spring of 2020, my career as a sommelier was upended. Restaurants closed because of the Covid-19 pandemic. My business shifted quickly to virtual events in a desperate effort to find much-needed community online. It was meant to be a pivot, and although it is still a work in progress, it has turned into something so much bigger than I ever could have dreamed. It hasn't been linear. In fact, when virtual events all but went away in the spring of 2022, a second shift became imperative. This unwanted pause also coincided with the most difficult time in my life. I don't believe that is a coincidence. As we grow and heal, we are given an opportunity to shift our mindset, to allow our healing to overflow into what is around us. When we begin to stand on a solid foundation, we give what we are building the opportunity to rest on that foundation too.

The table, which is the anchor for this book, is a place where people gather, where genuine community is felt, seen and experienced. It is also a metaphor for connectivity and intention, for gathering in authenticity. This book will be an exploration of life's tables and the richness of experience that is found there.

You will find a recipe and wine pairing at the beginning of each chapter. Each of these dishes are special to me in some way. They are my recipes or old family recipes. They are chosen and placed with intention as an invitation, an experience, to gather around your table in community.

Nannie's Seafood Gumbo (Creole)

This was my maternal grandma's, Bertha Jenkins', recipe. She was one of ten kids in rural Louisiana. She. Was. Tough. She used to say that "some things women are just better suited to handle than men." She taught me there can be great power in femininity.

Wine Pairing: Mosel or Nahe Kabinett Riesling

Ingredients

½ cup flour

½ cup oil

1 green bell pepper

2 celery stalks

1 white onion

2.25 lbs okra

1 12-oz can tomatoes

3 quarts stock

3 lbs shrimp peeled and deveined

1 lb lump crabmeat

Salt, black pepper, cayenne pepper to taste

Instructions

1. In a cast-iron skillet over high heat, heat the oil until it begins to smoke, then add the flour and whisk to make the roux, cook, whisking, 10-15 minutes or until medium chocolate brown.

2. Add the Holy Trinity: minced onion, celery, bell pepper. Sauté.

3. Add 12 oz of sliced okra and sauté.

4. Add the can of tomatoes.

5. Add the stock.

6. Season with salt, black pepper, cayenne to taste. Can add Cajun seasoning as well.

7. While the base is cooking, slice the rest of the okra and bake it in the oven at 350 degrees for 30 minutes. Add it into the base about an hour before the gumbo is finished.

8. Just before the gumbo is finished, after simmering for about 2-3 hours, let it come to a boil and add the seafood, cook for 10 minutes and serve over brown rice.

CHAPTER 1:

Setting the Table

I believe that setting a table is more than just placing forks and knives. It is an anticipatory gesture that is filled with romance and intention.

It says, "I thought of you, so I created something comfortable, something you would like," without saying a literal word. It is where food and wine are shared and community is built. It is where we come together as people, with all of our baggage and history and experiences, to just *be*. There is an authenticity found around the table that can't be matched anywhere else.

There is also a moment in a restaurant that comes just before the doors are open for service. A moment that is filled with intention. Setting the table is a gift to the guests who are coming. It is the calm before the storm. It is also when the staff has a moment to connect and commiserate. It is my absolute favorite time of the day because it is rife with connectivity and energy.

The table is a part of me on a soul level. I am an only child, which means a lot of things, but for me, it meant that my childhood was spent doing adult activities. We moved to California, forty-five minutes from Napa, when I was six. Wineries may not seem like the best place for kids, but for me, they were. For one, there is always at least one cat. There are trees to climb; and there is fruit to pick, depending upon the season—figs, citrus, apples or pears; and there are rows of vines to get lost in. I logged hours alone doing just that while my parents tasted and filled our old wood-paneled Dodge Caravan with wine. For my dad, wine was a status symbol. He had wines that were "around longer than Mom!" I knew where they were, and I knew not to touch them. They were like museum pieces, only to be adored from afar.

My parents grew up "poor" and "worked hard for all that they had." They weren't rich by California standards, but they were comfortable, and the presence of wine showed the world, and themselves, that they had *made it*. My dad loved the finer things. He loved to go to antique stores and buy fancy old plates and silver. He taught me how to set a proper table. You knew it was a nice meal when the crystal knife rests came out and the small crystal bowls with the tiny spoons that used to be used for drugs, but we used for salt, sat just above the forks. There was a romance in all of this that felt filled with intention—compiling tiny artifacts from other people's lives that had lived long before us and setting the table to share a meal.

My mom is from rural Louisiana, just outside of New Orleans. Her side of the family oozes hospitality. Food is their way of showing love. We went down there once a year. The itinerary was always comprised of "visitin'," which is a verb for stopping by people's houses unannounced and catching up. At each stop, there was food: gumbo, red beans and rice, king cake, Italian cream cake. Countless Southern women tried, unsuccessfully, to "put meat on my bones." There was a way that I felt in the South that differed from California. The passing of time didn't matter; I was loved and nourished and cared for, and food was the conduit. My mom made these staple dishes at home, but she also elevated her cooking. She's a rare breed of home cook that buys *The French Laundry* cookbook and actually makes things out of it. As I got older, I would help my dad pick the wine. He would ask me what went with duck, and I would reply, "Pinot!" well before I could legally drive.

Despite food taking such a center stage in my childhood home, I was an insanely picky eater. I was a quiet observer, keen to see how others did things, but less inclined to jump in myself. This was certainly the case as far as food was concerned. The table was still a gathering place, but if everyone else was having duck à l'orange, I was happily mowing down mac 'n' cheese.

When I was fifteen, my parents took me to Paris, a trip that changed me at my core. They were still on the French franc at the time, so the dollar went *far*. We dined in some of the most beautiful restaurants I have ever seen. I had wine paired with food for the first time. I was mesmerized by how you could take one thing that was good, put it with something else that was also good, and create a new flavor that was extraordinary. It was magic, pure and simple. Beyond that, I experienced service for the first time. Waiters, elegantly adorned in tuxedos, stood with their hands behind their backs, waiting to get us anything we needed. The way they seemed to glide through the space was intoxicating. I was a dancer, and this was better than any ballet I had ever seen. I came home from that trip knowing that this is what I wanted to spend my life doing. So upon our return, I got a job at the only white-tablecloth restaurant in town. The love affair began. I became one of those waiters for many, many years, and I absolutely *loved* it.

Beef Wellington

When I went away to college, my mom gave me a notebook with handwritten "easy" recipes. This was the first entry. We still laugh about it because what college kid has access to foie gras or the ability to make beef wellington in their dorm room? I am sure this dish was served more than once at the Gourmet Group, detailed in the upcoming chapter.

Wine Pairing: Northern Rhône Red like St. Joseph or Côte Rôtie if you want to be as fancy as this dish

Ingredients
1 lb beef filet
1 sheet puff pastry
1 can pâté de foie gras (alternatively, you can substitute the foie gras for sautéed minced shallots with diced mushrooms)
1 egg
Maldon salt

Instructions
1. After seasoning with Maldon salt, brown the filet on all sides in a cast-iron skillet over high heat, roast in the oven at 450 degrees for 15 minutes for medium rare. Take out and let it rest on a cutting board.

2. Roll out the puff pastry on a floured board to about ⅛ inch thick. Spread the pâté on an area large enough to cover the meat.

3. Place the meat top side down on the pastry and wrap.

4. Seal with egg wash made with 1 beaten egg.

5. Save some pastry to make a lattice design on the top. Fasten with egg wash and brush egg wash over the surface of the top of the pastry.

6. Bake at 450 degrees for 30 minutes or until golden brown.

7. Slice and serve.

CHAPTER 2:

Evolving at The Table

As a kid, I always found myself to be the only child at the table with grownups. Being an only child meant I was often brought along to dinner parties and restaurants. An old family friend told me recently that I was just a "tiny grownup" back then. I wasn't; I had just learned to perform early on. As a family, we gathered around the table every night to share a meal. My dad loved to connect and hear what I was up to.

"What are you working on?" was often a question I heard. My dad loved to problem-solve. It was the fuel that lit his fire, both personally and professionally, so our dinnertime discussions often led to solving problems I didn't even know that I had. This outlook made me begin to look at the world this way: What problems can I solve? What can I do to make things better, easier, more efficient?

When we are born, the elemental people in our lives imprint upon us. When we succeed, they are the first to clap. When we fail, the weight of the disappointment in their eyes is unbearable. We begin to define our successes and failures by what we are met with at the table. What energy is there? All kids want positive reinforcement, but they don't get that 100 percent of the time.

Maria Shriver, in her book *Maria,* describes her family table as a place where people only talked about how they were going to change the world. She had a huge legacy to live up to, the Kennedys, her father starting the Peace Corps, running for president, and her mother starting the Special Olympics in their backyard. Because of this, she struggled to know who she was outside of her accomplishments, to carve out an identity for herself apart from the gold stars she hung on the mantel. In an effort to impress, we often spend this sacred time around the table listing our wins or discussing our failures only to be met with reactions that either encourage or suppress us. The early years at the table are paramount for defining who we become later in life.

The same was true for me. My parents both worked corporate jobs for Chevron for nearly sixty years combined. They had a group called the Gourmet Group, which met monthly with friends who also loved nice meals paired with wine. Each family would be responsible for a course for their themed dinners. All of the couples were younger than my parents, so for a very long time, I was the only kid at the table. Much of my childhood was spent unknowingly performing, learning how to read the cues of others, and showing up how they expected me to.

All members of the *Gourmet Group* worked together, so by default, they spoke in acronyms I didn't understand, talking about what "level" jobs certain coworkers had. I understood, even then, that your level was a mere projection of your success in an organization designed with structured intent. In my current career and life iteration, I have flashbacks to these moments. Today, I serve corporate clients directly, which means I am still in the room as many acronyms are thrown around. I still find myself feeling like the only kid at the big table, surrounded by a foreign but familiar language filled with acronyms and pleasantries. The discomfort of the familiar is not lost on me.

It makes sense then, that the feeling of openness and acceptance in the restaurant business has always been the draw for me. Restaurant people are decidedly, if not proudly, fringe. The "us" and "them" mentality goes a long way when building morale and making people feel as if they're really a part of something. Show up exactly how you are. The slightly performative nature in fine dining restaurants acts as a protective layer or shield from the outside world. Perhaps a strange thing to hear when the job is so public-facing, when we truly put our souls on the line every night in service. The restaurant business serves this inward community by being a safe place for the "others" to land.

There is a commonality between people who land in restaurants for life. Their stories might be different, but the needs they are looking to fill are the same. Even at the highest level, they are often deep feelers and have a big life event or struggle that propels them into a life of service. Will Guidara, author of *Unreasonable Hospitality,* discusses his mom's terminal illness when he was in high school in his book. He details dining at Daniel in New York City just after his mother's inevitable passing from brain cancer as providing a "ray of light during a terribly dark time." What struck me most about the scene he painted is that often we think of restaurants as being places for celebrating life's milestones, but they can also be places where we receive unforgettable generosity during our darkest moments in life. This part of his book brought me to tears because I related on a soul level to the way restaurants can act as a cocoon during life's most painful moments. Master Sommelier Bobby Stuckey struggled with dyslexia before discovering his life's purpose: bussing tables. Bobby is one of the most successful restaurateurs in the country, as well as a Master Sommelier, but he proudly says, "Once a busboy, always a busboy." In his recent James Beard acceptance speech, he highlighted that the restaurant world is a place for people to land who have "made mistakes, don't speak the language, single parents who need a flexible schedule." Restaurants are a landing place for the sensitive souls that don't feel like they belong in the structured world with everyone else.

I got my first restaurant job when I was fifteen, after that trip to Paris. The romanticized story I tell, the one you just read, is real, but there was something else happening in conjunction that propelled me into the hospitality world. My childhood home was filled with a ton of love. It also became a really sad place to be, literally overnight. Just before the end of my eighth-grade year, my father was diagnosed with a brain tumor. He wasn't supposed to see me graduate from high school. He underwent brain surgery right away, and then they blasted him with chemo and radiation. He would have periods of health, but mostly, they nuked him, and I had a front-row seat. Prior to that fateful day in 1996, my dad was my protector and my guide. He went from being the strongest person I knew to needing help getting up off the bathroom floor when he was sick from chemo. My parents relied on me to be their light in the dark. I took that responsibility very seriously. Making them happy at all costs was my focus. Be the court jester, their source of joy. The dining room floor of a restaurant became a place where I couldn't feel feelings. Perhaps it felt comfortable because of the performative nature at home, but I got that first restaurant job to have a place to escape. What I didn't realize was that I would find my community there.

I spent the next twenty-five years using the floor of the restaurant as a place to be someone else. Back then, work gave me a reason to be out of the house. There was also an obvious line I could draw from earning money to achieving the freedom necessary to escape the heaviness that had infested the walls of my childhood home. I fit into the restaurant world because I could put on a mask and transform into an entirely different person. When guests come in night after night, they have an expectation. They expect to see you the same, day after day, positive and full of light. People don't feel the same day after day. We go through cycles. Some days we are down; others we are over the moon. In restaurants, in service, on the floor, you must be consistent. I think this is why there is so much army jargon in restaurants because consistency over feelings is paramount. It is almost as if your life depends upon it.

The performative aspect of this dance was learned and then rewarded. More times than I can count, I went from my dad's bedside at a hospital directly into service. It was a massive distraction. When you are busy yourself, you aren't able to feel feelings. I would learn later in life that the key to actually healing from our pain comes with sitting with ourselves, without distraction, but my younger years were spent building the mask, the armor, the protection. The restaurant was where I could dump my feelings, leave them at the door, if only for a brief moment in time. The restaurant was where I felt safe. As soon as I walked back out into the world, the weight would come back. By running there to escape all of those years, I admittedly kicked a lot of healing down the road, but the job came first. I think that's natural when we are young, when we are striving for our goals. When we are so focused on achievements, we are always looking ahead to the future, and we forget to truly experience the moment we are in.

Ken Burns and Anderson Cooper discuss work as their default mode as early as twelve after Burns lost his mother and Cooper lost his father. Working is a really easy way to get lost in the "busy," to escape the grief we might be feeling. It might seem odd to look at a diagnosis as the start of a grieving journey, but it is. The person I had always known as my dad had shifted, changed somehow, with the knowing that he wasn't immortal. We lost a piece of him, ever so subtly, when we got that diagnosis. What we didn't know was that we would spend the next twenty-eight years watching him slowly slip away and fight back again and again in real time.

In high school, my love for restaurants deepened quickly, despite the first chef I worked with angrily calling me "romper room" every time I made a mistake, which was often. My friend group at the time was reminiscent of the Lost Boys, a group of kids that were on the fringe, often turning to drugs and drinking to escape. I proudly took on my role as Wendy, mothering and nurturing my peers as if they were my own children. I didn't know it, but caring for others was one way that I nurtured the parts of me that were desperate to be cared for. My dream was to go to the University of Colorado Boulder so I could ski, but my parents nudged me to a soon-to-be-major at San Diego State University (SDSU): hospitality and tourism management.

SDSU in the early 2000s was exactly what you'd imagine it to be. Somehow, through sheer will and determination, I graduated in four and a half years only attending classes on Tuesdays and Thursdays so I could work the other days. I was always an average student, mostly because my social life came first, but also because, to this day, I hyperfocus on the things that bring me joy while giving little to no time to things that I don't find interesting. Once I got into my major, I excelled. I ended up graduating with the highest GPA of our little restaurant subset. There were four of us, but I was still proud.

Throughout college, I always had a restaurant job. Most were mediocre establishments at best, which continuously made me question my life choices. One fine establishment was so beachfront that we would have to arrive early to shovel rocks off the patio that the sea brought up after storms. The carpet was hunter green. There was a lot of brass. We used tray jacks and giant banquet trays. We, the waiters, would drink the bottomless mimosas while we served brunch and would try to outdo each other with how many times we could say "meow" at the table without our guests noticing. *Super Troopers* had just come out, and it was a *thing*. The manager was wildly addicted to cocaine and did a terrible job hiding it. Despite working for lunatics, I always worked. One summer, I got my first job as a prep cook. I loved the kitchen. I would arrive early, 7:30 a.m., and get to work. It was a busy restaurant in La Jolla that was open for lunch, so prep came first before working the line for a busy lunch service. My day in the kitchen would wrap around 2:30 p.m., and I would drive north to Del Mar to bartend and wait tables at night. That shift started at 3:30 p.m., and with traffic, I would often transform myself into a different person in full glam while on the 405. I was young, but even so, working nineteen-hour days five days a week was energizing, mostly because the kitchen was a place where I was learning all day long and being challenged. The front of the house, to this day, feels like putting on a soft pair of pajamas. It's easy, like coming home. Despite being nudged by one of my professors to stay in San Diego post-graduation, I knew the real restaurant industry at the time was in San Francisco. I knew I needed to go home if I was going to have an actual career in this business.

Before delving headfirst into my career, I had to satisfy a little wanderlust. As soon as I graduated, I packed up everything I owned into a U-Haul, dumped it in a storage unit, packed two suitcases, and moved to England for culinary school. I was craving adventure and a big change. I had visited a friend in Paris over spring break and fell in love with the idea of studying abroad. I had also gotten a taste of working in the kitchen by then, a tight-knit community that felt thick as thieves. The front of the house was always built of an amalgamation of people with storied histories who had a propensity for drama. The back of the house, the cooks, were heads-down, get-it-done people. Even in the throes of a busy stressful service, they never faltered, rarely lost their cool. They got it done, and I respected that. Chefs were a unique breed of human. They were not put together, or stuffy, or elegant. They were a mess, and I loved them too. It always amazed me how the people responsible for creating those incredible dishes were the misfits, the ones that don't fit into normal society. It was a club I was happy to be a part of. It was a club that felt like those old Southern women of my childhood. It was a club that made me feel loved.

Culinary school ended up being a gateway for travel. I arrived on a Tuesday, and by Thursday night I was bartending at a high-end bar up the street from my apartment. The women I worked with became my community, my closest friends. I couldn't afford to dine out, but each night, at the end of our busy shift, we would sit around the table before we deep-cleaned the bar. We would eat a meal from the chip shop, drink beer, smoke cigarettes, and talk. This shared space felt sacred, a way to come down after a busy service. Bartending at night meant that I could also save the little money I made and use it toward travel. I would look up the cheapest bus tickets or plane flights in Europe to determine my itinerary. I stayed in hostels, ate baguettes and jars of olives for meals, and really got to *see* the world. I was free in a way I had never been. I ended up backpacking alone through Europe for about six months with no cell phone, nothing but a *Lonely Planet* guidebook and a one-disc CD player with one mixed CD that the boyfriend I left behind had made for me. Being an only child makes me good at being alone, but this was *really* alone. Days would pass where I wouldn't speak simply because I never ran into anyone else who spoke English. When you travel in this way, you truly give yourself up to the kindness of strangers, to whatever is in store for you. It was a lonely time in my life, but was so profoundly beautiful.

I remember having a phone conversation one night after working a busy shift at the bar, that was maybe one of the most impactful conversations of my life. It was finally approaching summer, which meant that the light hung a little longer in the UK. I would go to work when the sun was out and would finish my shift as it rose. Working through the night can be pretty disorienting. I got home to my fifth floor walk-up apartment, ready to shower and go to sleep when I realized the water in the building had been shut off. I sat on the floor and had a good, deep cry. I bundled myself back up and went down to the payphone in the courtyard and called home. I was painfully lonely, but hearing my dad's voice on the other end of the line felt like light in the dark.

"Hi, sweetheart, how are you doing?" The tears flowed. The weight of being in another country, so far from home, was heavy and difficult to move through. I also knew that when I came home, it would be time to figure out what I was going to do professionally. There was a lot of pressure, both internal and external, put on this decision. We talked it through, and at one point, my dad said something that has stayed with me.

He said, "If you choose something you love, it won't feel like work. I love problem-solving and finding ways to save Chevron money. I love my job. Yours might look different, but just choose what you love." That energy, moving toward what lights you up, has been a north star throughout my life. Even in his very logical, left-brained mind, my dad was still a living example of moving from his heart.

The interesting thing is that my dad was both a guiding force, my biggest champion and best mentor early on, while also reigning supreme. That control made me feel stifled, stuck in place. The restaurant business liberated me somehow, brought connections from faraway places without leaving home, all while pacifying him by making him proud.

When I ran out of money, I moved home begrudgingly. I had asked for a one-way ticket initially, but my parents said no, knowing all too well that if they complied, they would likely never see me again. I had no money, just a mountain of college and travel debt.

I moved back in with my folks and got two jobs doing what I did best: waiting tables.

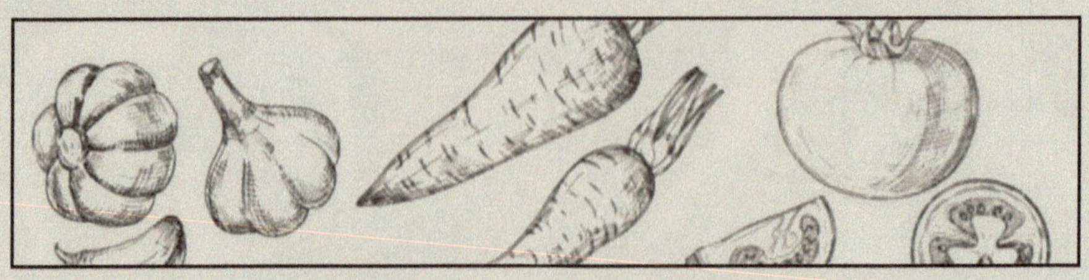

24-Hour Bolognese

I make a huge batch of this pasta sauce every few weeks and pull out a single serving a week to have for dinner. It is a staple in our house. The broth is super important, so I've detailed how to make the perfect stock below.

Wine Pairing: Barolo or Barbaresco

Ingredients

1 lb ground pork
1 lb ground beef
Maldon salt
1 16-oz can of tomato
1 yellow onion
4 cloves garlic minced

2 diced carrots
1 cup white wine
1 cup red wine
4 cups broth
Olive oil

Instructions

1. Season the ground beef and pork with Maldon salt and brown in olive oil over high heat, remove and set aside.
2. Add the diced onion and carrot into the same pot and sauté over medium heat until translucent.
3. Add the minced garlic and sauté for another few minutes.
4. Add the browned meat back into the pot along with the tomatoes, red and white wine, and broth.
5. Simmer on low heat for 24 hours, adding stock as needed, reduce to sauce consistency to finish.
6. Add fresh thyme and salt to taste.
7. This makes a huge batch, so just take what you need into a sauté pan. Cook your pasta in salted water until al dente. Add the pasta, along with a splash of pasta water into the sauté pan with more olive oil, reduce the water out so the sauce coats the pasta.
8. Serve with Parmesan cheese.

Broth: I make my broth with all of our leftover bones from the week—a chicken carcass, pork bones, plus 2-3 chicken feet, plus about ¼ cup of apple cider vinegar. You can use an Instant Pot if you run on Meat/Stew for three 3-hour sessions. You'll get a dark, rich broth. Stovetop with the lid on works as well, but you'll need to simmer for 24+ hours to get a flavorful stock.

CHAPTER 3

The Table as a Grounding Force for Love

The first half of my adult life was spent being supported and raised by the community I met within the four walls of whatever fine dining establishment I found myself in. I found my people in restaurants. I also found love.

After my European wanderings, I landed at À Côté, a little Bohemian enclave that sits on the border of Oakland and Berkeley. The gentleman who ran it had the largest impact on the trajectory of my life, hands down. Jeff Berlin embodies love and is larger than life. He came down for my interview in a Grateful Dead tie-dye t-shirt, shorts, and Birkenstocks, looked at my resume, and asked when I could start. Jeff has an uncanny ability to create culture just by being. He was our fearless leader, but he was more than that. He made that space ooze love and connection from every corner. He worked there for nearly twenty years, and when he left, the soul left with him. He has a gift. He also loves wine. When he taught, he would transport us to those far-off places, the places I longed for from my travels. He would speak about Pigato, which comes from the coastal towns of Liguria. The vines hang over the Mediterranean and are drenched in sunlight and sea air. When I put my nose in the glass, I could smell it. I was there.

His wine list was entirely European and incredibly esoteric.

People would come in and say, "I want a California Zinfandel."

To which I would reply, "Well, I have Plavac Mali from Croatia, which is an ancient relative of Primativo from Puglia, which is an ancient relative of Zinfandel!" Most of the people that live on the Oakland/Berkeley border are open and well-traveled, so to my surprise, they took my suggestions. I was told countless stories from guests about their trips to this region or that. I could commiserate because I too had just been in that small village in that faraway place and had a similar experience. I began to see how wine not only connected people but also had the ability to transport you to a different time and place.

Before you have a deeper relationship with wine, you could argue that it is just booze you can use to escape. The reality is that your sense memory is directly tied to how you feel and perceive the world around you. It is uniquely yours. When people tell me that a wine smells "like my grandma's basement," I'm like, "Yes! Tell me about your grandma!"

There is a way that our shoulders come down, that we ease into a space when wine acts as the anchor. A shared experience, yet entirely unique, that leaves us unguarded and open to possibility. There is a reason that wine has graced tables for millennia. À Côté was an education like no other, an immersion into a world where wine connected us despite our differences. Here, in this creative space, is where I met my husband. He was a wine sales person that tried to dress up in argyle sweaters, but they always had holes. He played guitar, was brilliant and charming, so it was clear from the start that this was *my guy*.

When you began working at À Côté, it didn't matter what kind of experience you had, you started by running the door. Ironically, hostess was the only position I hadn't yet added to my resumé. Thankfully, Jeff was of the mindset that the more champagne you drank, the better host you became. At that point in my life, I was of that mindset too.

I arrived early on my first day, wearing a white bohemian skirt, a pink spaghetti-strapped top, and heels. I climbed the stairs up to the treehouse-like office that sat above the restaurant. In the room were two people: Jeff and a baby-faced dark-haired guy with icy blue eyes.

"This is Sean," was met with, "Hey, nice to meet you," as I settled into the office chair to print the menus. He was *cute*. I kept my eyes locked on the screen. I would come to learn that this "Sean" was fresh out of a five-year relationship with someone he'd *lived* with. At that point, the only members of the opposite sex I had lived with were from the summer I moved into a frat house so I wouldn't have to go home to the Bay Area in between leases. He sold wine, and lived practically next door, so he was in and out of the restaurant a lot, often when we were setting up for service. He would come in, I would notice, and immediately my stomach would drop or my heart would skip a beat, and I would quickly avert my eyes to the napkins I was folding.

Traveling alone in Europe and landing back in Oakland meant that this was a transitory time that was met with a little social anxiety. I had to ease back into the world post-wanderlust. He knew everyone at the restaurant; it was a place he could show off, so he also brought a few dates in. The women I worked with knew I had a crush on him but told me not to worry about it because he "needed time to get over his ex." One night, he came in with his ex and her brother. It was his birthday. I took the table. The ex ordered an El Pepino, which was this delicious cucumber gin cocktail we had on the menu, but she didn't seem like she was having a good time. It felt forced, like they showed up out of obligation. I dropped the check, and they were gone quickly. I felt defeated. He left with her. That's it. I quickly envisioned their entire impending wedding.

A few minutes later, I spotted him at the end of the bar, alone. I took a deep breath and walked up to him and told him we were going to the dive bar down the street after work and invited him along. I was the closer, so I was off last. He seemed to be waiting for me. By the time my shift was over, he had been drinking for many hours. We walked as a group up College Ave. Someone grabbed a scarf off the ground and wrapped it around the birthday boy's neck. Fernet Branca was a shared love of ours early on, and many Fernets later, we all ended up back at Sean's house. We smoked hookah, and he played guitar. At one point, I was sitting behind him on the couch. He was on the rug in front of me, and he laid his head back onto my lap.

Years later, a mutual friend told me that Sean said, "When I laid my head on her lap, I felt like I had just come home." When I went into work the next day, there was a brown paper bag on the back bar with my name on it. I opened it, and the scarf was inside with a note—"I thought it was all a dream, but then I found this scarf"— and his number. I waited the obligatory two days to call him.

On our first date, my dad gave me a bottle of 1981 Carneros Creek Cabernet to impress him. Old wine offers its own level of magic. Wine, like people, becomes more authentic as it ages, more true to the place from which it comes. Cabernet is a primary example. When it is young, it is brazen, bold, and flashy, but as it spends time in the bottle, the fruit falls out, the wine softens, and the minerality shines through. It's reminiscent of being driven by ego when we are younger and building a mask, to slowly letting all of that go and allowing our pure authenticity to shine through unobstructed.

That first date with Sean was easy. It truly did feel like coming home. We ate three dinners in a row and drank a tremendous amount of wine. Late into the night, sitting at a table at À Côté, where we decided to go for a cheese plate and a nightcap bottle of Sancerre Rosé, we were quiet. I thought to myself, *This is a person I am comfortable just* being *with*. There was no need to fill space with words, no nervous energy, just ease. We quickly began spending any free time we had together.

The more time I spent in restaurants, the more I realized that wine and food were storytelling devices. The more I knew, the longer I could stay at the table and the richer the experiences I could create. It was a way to engage people for longer, to connect them through what was in the glass to the people and the places, rich in history and culture, without leaving the restaurant. I became obsessed with knowing all that I could about wine.

Sean would come home from work most days with bags of opened wine from appointments. Tasting is such a fundamental part of wine education. You can memorize how wine is made, regions and subregions, soil types and types of oak, climate and viticulture, but it's the act of connecting all of that knowledge to what is in the glass that makes it all come together. It brings purpose to the study. It was an amazing education. He also knew more than me, and I *liked him,* so I had to catch up. I spent my days at cafés before work drawing maps of wine regions and making flashcards. I was a sponge, and this was the only thing that mattered. I took exams and received accreditations, but my connection to wine deepened in an unexpected way. It was not only a connecting point, but it brought together history, weather, climate, geography, geology, cuisine, and people. Countless winemakers from Europe flocked to À Côté to host wine dinners. We would drink and eat with them until the sun came up. I was in another club, a club that transported me all over the world without having to leave Oakland. I was hooked.

It was very early in our relationship, but there was something in Sean that felt familiar, like he wasn't a stranger, or like this wasn't the first time we'd done this. I wouldn't call it love at first sight. It's far deeper and more complex than that, but it was like we knew each other already. Before we even went on our official first date, we sat on his porch and drank coffee. We talked about all of the off-limit things. I remember thinking to myself, *Oh, he's here. He's not supposed to be here yet. I have so many things to do first, but okay.*

I had plans to pay off my debt and save enough to move to South America next. I wanted to learn the language, live with a family, and really immerse myself in the culture. I spoke a lot about leaving in those early days. After a couple months of dating, I found a month-to-month studio apartment off of Piedmont Avenue in Oakland. It was tiny. My rent was $650 a month, but it was *mine.* I had never lived alone, and even though Sean and I spent every night together, it felt quiet in my little studio. After about a month, I ended up on Sean's porch, just before my shift at À Côté, with a tiny six-week-old gray kitten. This sweet kitten sparked the conversation that took our relationship to the next level. The apartment didn't scare him, he didn't bat an eye at spending every night together, but that cat? That meant this was serious.

"I thought you were leaving," he said, shocked as he looked at her sweet little face. Little did he know about the countless other furry creatures I had pawned off on my parents when the itch to go became relentless.

"I am leaving, but I'm here now," was all I could think to respond with. That little kitty made us realize that what we were building was worth staying for, that sometimes, when the right person comes into your life, you choose to shift course to accommodate them for no other reason than you can't imagine going on without them. It was so early in our journey, and we were so insanely young, but we knew that whatever we did, we wanted to do it together.

Sean is an empath and a wise, wise soul. He is a healer and a guide and someone I am immensely grateful to call my partner. He is a brilliant musician. He is intuitive. He sees people without them saying a literal word. He has an insane gift for connection and is adored by everyone who meets him. He is my mentor and guide in so many ways. I have learned more from him than anyone else. We've walked through the trenches together, and we've had the highest of highs. True partnership must be tested and tried on the most rigorous of levels. To walk alongside him is a gift I am so profoundly grateful for and is a privilege I do not take lightly.

I began to see that wine attracted a certain type of person, one who embodies love, not romantic love, but open-heartedness and acceptance. In 2006, we saved up the money we had, and we planned our first wine trip. We went to Piedmont, in northwestern Italy. Because he sold wine, we were given a house to stay in, in a vineyard, for free by a generations-old winemaking family. It was rustic, but this was a far cry from the hostel travels of my recent past. One late afternoon, we met with Luca Currado from Vietti. Luca comes from a long line of winemakers: six generations to be exact. He wore a brightly colored sweater and jeans. He told animated stories with his hands. He showed us where his father hid wine from the Nazis during the war, in the walls under the church of La Morra, and then he and his wife, Elena, took us to dinner.

On the windy roads on the rolling hills of vineyards dotted with castles, a song came on the radio. Luca grabbed his phone, made a call, turned up the radio, and he and Elena sang their hearts out. It was a pop song, and they were having the *best* time. When he hung up, he looked back at us and said in his thick Italian accent, "This is our daughter's favorite song!" They had to call to share the moment with her.

When we arrived for dinner, I ordered bagna càuda upon Elena's insistence, and we went to the cellar to pick the wine. Luca's family had lived in La Morra for generations, and this restaurant had likely been in this place for just as long, so the number of times he had visited this cellar, one can only imagine to be in the thousands. I watched his face light up like a child on Christmas morning. It was infectious. He danced around the massive cellar showing us where everything was stored. When you study wine, these places and these people become like celebrities, but we were *here*, we were with *them*, and they were *human*. He picked the wine, and we went back upstairs to the table. They opened a 1982 Aldo Conterno Bussia Barolo, a wine I had only read about that came from a producer I idolized and a favorite vineyard, but was well out of my economic reach. The wine was unlike anything I had ever experienced. It was incredible. I couldn't help but think that Aldo himself had likely walked that case over to this cellar in 1986 or so, just after It was bottled, and it hadn't moved since. Luca and Elena began speaking in Italian to each other for a bit.

Elena looked up and said, "We were just discussing where we were in 1982 and what we were doing." Then she paused and looked at me and said, "Oh, it's your birth year, isn't it?" It was. This was an average Tuesday night for them, but for me, it was a moment imprinted on my memory and my life that I will never forget. We have stayed connected with them, and so many like them, throughout our careers. It doesn't matter when or where we see him, Luca lights up like a kid on Christmas, grabs our faces and kisses us. He, like so many others in this business, is **LOVE.**

Coq au Vin

This is an easy dish to prepare. I will often substitute chicken for rabbit. It feels warm and inviting and is perfect for a fall night at home.

Wine Pairing: Cru Beaujolais like Morgon or Fleurie

Ingredients

1 whole chicken or rabbit
1 lb chanterelle mushrooms
1 onion diced
2 cloves of garlic
3 cups broth (see 24-Hour
　Bolognese recipe in chapter 3 for
　stock instructions)

1 cup red wine
1 cup white wine
Fresh thyme, sage, or whatever
　you got!
Maldon salt

Instructions

1. Sauté the mushrooms in the pan with olive oil and salt until the water evaporates and set aside.

2. Break down the rabbit or chicken so you have the two legs, breasts, and wings separated. Salt with Maldon.

3. Brown the meat over high heat in the pan you intend to use for the dish. Once browned on all sides, remove the meat and set aside.

4. Reduce the heat and add the diced onion to the pan and cook until translucent, then add the minced garlic and stir for about a minute.

5. Put the chicken or rabbit back into the pot and add the stock and the wine, simmer for 30 minutes, pull the meat out so it doesn't fall apart and turn up the heat to reduce liquid into a more sauce or stew like consistency, salt to taste.

6. Add the mushroom and the meat back in.

7. Finish with fresh herbs.

8. Serve with pommes purée, polenta, or rice.

CHAPTER 4:

Found Family Through Service

Restaurants brought an entire cast of characters to my table, my community, my people. I would be a completely different person if it weren't for restaurants, which are a fundamental part of society, gathering places that build community by welcoming guests and feeding them, which is one of the richest ways we show love. They also serve an internal community, a dysfunctional family unit of sorts. Whether it's a Michelin starred restaurant or a diner, the restaurant business attracts a similar personality type: deep feelers that crave human connection and feel whole when serving others.

I read *Adventures on the Wine Route* by Kermit Lynch when I was twenty-two and absolutely loved it. I managed a small restaurant at the time where I was allowed to buy a little wine for the wine list. I had a tasting appointment at Kermit's shop in Berkeley. I spent my time there gushing over the book, tasting a few things, and buying a few cases for the restaurant. In the car on the way home, they called me and asked me if I wanted to work there. "YES!" couldn't come out fast enough. I spent about six months with no days off. My two days a week not working in the restaurant were spent on the retail floor at Kermit.

One of the perks of working for Kermit was that he would have us over to his house for dinner about once a month. I will never forget my first time in his Berkeley home. Dark wood, stained glass windows, and the smell of coq au vin wafted from the kitchen. I was handed a glass of white wine. I put my nose in the glass and was transported to the seaside, the Mendocino coast at low tide, to be exact. The smell of the tide pools ... saline and salty sea air. What.

Was. This? It turned out it was my first experience with Raveneau: the 1979 Les Clos, an unmistakable Grand Cru that smells like the salty sea as it ages. We sat for dinner, and a magnum came around. It smelled like my grandmother's violet perfume, cured meat, and dark berry fruit: 1982 Chave Hermitage, my birth year. I am lucky to have had several "pinch me" moments in my career, but this was one that stood out in a major way. The warmth of his home, balanced by two of the most iconic wines in the world, all enjoyed in community, in the least pretentious way imaginable. The old Southern women of my past were coming back, this time in Berkeley California.

The love and inclusion I felt in the world of wine propelled me deeper into my studies and made me steadfast in my desire to become a sommelier. I was twenty-four when I walked into an iconic San Francisco restaurant, which was known for its incredible wine collection, paper resume in hand. The previous owner and wine director had built the cellar from the ground up. She was the first person to bring Austrian wine to San Francisco. We had a Brundlymeyer Grüner Veltliner from 1983 that cost the restaurant $14 a bottle. The cellar was hers, and she was an icon in my eyes. I had the privilege of opening and sharing renowned wines that I had only read about. That cellar gave me access for the first time. She hired some of the best women in the business as well.

Today, I am thankful to call these women my friends, but then, I felt the weight of those that came before me in that space. Being a female sommelier was relatively rare at that point.

I was often met with, "Are you even old enough to pour this wine?" I knew that what they faced was harder. Those who carve a path for others are always met with greater hardship, but it was my job to carry the torch. I often found myself in roles early on where, although I was fanatically studying wine, I would look around and be like, *I can't know the MOST out of all of these people.* This combination of factors plus my own internal dialogue made me unsure through most of my career if I was even meant to be there, if I was good enough. That internal struggle was the catalyst in the early years for me to prove myself.

I was hired by an industry veteran. He was a tortured soul that often spoke of his abusive alcoholic mother and absentee father. He was soft and sweet and a big feeler, but you could see how the circumstances of his life had hardened him. The blackness of his eyes, mostly due to his abundant use of cocaine, had a softness behind them. When he took time off from the restaurant, which was *rare,* he would travel to far off places like Vietnam or Nepal, rent a motorcycle, and go far and wide. His drug addiction became more apparent as time went on. The only thing that could bring him down during service was a South African Sauvignon Blanc—a $4 bottle of wine we used for happy hour. He would keep a bottle stashed near the well for easy access, dumped into a rocks glass and consumed throughout the night. One time I counted four bottles in one evening. There was a delicate balance for him between wine and cocaine. When the two meshed well, he was charming and ran the dining room floor with ease. When one or the other overtook him, so did his demons. He would lurk around the dining room with his arms folded across his concave chest, his black eyes darting around the room like a cornered feral cat. I would offer to close for him on those nights because I worried he was creeping out the guests. Despite his own trauma, he never yelled, never escalated issues beyond calm conversation. The best restaurant professionals are the deepest feelers; he only used to escape the weight of his.

All chefs pretend that they don't like to speak in front of people, that they're introverts that would prefer to hide behind the safety of the kitchen doors. The first chef at this restaurant had a "please don't make me be on stage" act, but the minute you handed him a glass of champagne, he'd swoop his imaginary hair over his shoulder and saunter out on the floor with ease. He was loud, relatively good-looking as far as chefs go, and charming. He could cook, and he knew it. His office was located on the roof of the restaurant. It had a couch and a fur rug. I never went in there, mostly because I was well aware of his girlfriend, who would always show up during service. "Where's Chef?" was met with diverted eyes. That office had seen more than I was willing to. Bro-code went far for him, especially when his wife and children would show up at the restaurant, often missing *her* by mere minutes. It was gross, but he knew we had his back.

The second chef I worked with at this restaurant was quiet, a true introvert, and so kind. That said, he had a rage inside of him that I hadn't seen in a chef in a long time. One New Year's Eve, we got busy, too busy really. The restaurant was massive, and when it was sat at full capacity with a tasting menu, it was all any of us could do to keep up.

I was on the third floor mezzanine when I heard him screaming at the line cook at the sauté station at top of his lungs: "ARE YOU FUCKING UNEDUCATED?!?! JUST PLATE THE FUCKING CHICKENNNNN!!!!!" I made a joke to my table who also heard him clear as day, and quickly floated down the stairs to the kitchen. When my eyes met his, I saw absolute carnage: the board, the area that holds the tickets, was full, the machine was still printing, and the tickets attached to it were draped over chef's broad six-foot-plus frame and down the other side, making a pile onto the floor by his right foot. "Fuck," I muttered out loud to no one in particular. I ran to the bar, poured a double shot of something brown, and placed it on the line in front of Chef without saying a word. It was a bold move that could have easily been met with further rage, but it was my attempt at saying, "I've got you ... we'll get through this together." He understood. I spent the next few hours pouring extra pours of wine, telling stories, trying to distract our guests from the absurd amount of time it was taking to get their dinner. I never heard him yell like that again. He and I developed an unspoken bond. We were on the tail end of that restaurant. As they began to trim costs, we would close the restaurant together. We would cut the staff as early as possible to save labor dollars.

One night, as he was cleaning the kitchen and I was relighting pilot lights on the line, I remember him saying, "Do you think Mario fucking Batali is shutting down garde manger right now?! I don't fucking think so ... what the actual fuck?!" Despite the absurdity of our newfound custodial roles, we complied with grace. When you're young, and you deeply believe in what you are doing, you'll do just about anything for the cause. Martyrdom is rewarded in the restaurant business. Sacrificing self, historically, was not only expected but celebrated. The more we gave our lives to the business we were running, the better we looked and the better we felt. I relied so heavily on external praise in those days that not conforming to what was expected was not even an option.

The front of house staff was also thick as thieves, mostly because they partied together until the sun came up every night at after-hour underground clubs in the Haight. They would roll into work at 3 p.m. looking rough most days. Blackened eyes filled with joy, rehashing stories from the night before as we set the dining room for service. I was younger than most of them at twenty-four, but had just bought my first house and was planning my wedding. I was focused on checking life's boxes, so my goals for life and work kept me steadfast. In retrospect, I always thought my dad was going to die, so I felt like I needed to meet certain milestones so he could see them. He was so important to me that I didn't want him to miss it, a subtle weighing of obligation to hurry up and get there, to achieve traditionally defined success as soon as possible. When I did go out with them, I was met with surprise and always left before the really naughty things came out. I loved them like family. They were true professionals, had encyclopedic knowledge of food and wine, and despite being massively hungover most days, could always perform.

This place was also *the* San Francisco wine restaurant of the '90s, complete with an underground jazz bar and an amazing wine cellar. I started in 2007, so I was on the tail end of the restaurant's life, which is always a challenging place to come in. You can feel the presence of the people that came before you in the space, but the space itself starts to feel tired, like it's struggling to keep up. The restaurant was a cavernous warehouse with multiple floors. It felt lived in. It also came with many regulars. The thing about regulars in restaurants is that you often see them more than your own family. You grow to love them. The type of person that bellies up to the bar multiple nights a week may not present on the outside as someone who struggles, but they do. They come with their history and their complexities. They too are deeply searching for connection.

One of my favorite regulars was the famous photographer Jim Marshall. He was the only photographer at Folsom Prison the day Johnny Cash famously flipped the bird. He is responsible for taking the photos of The Beatles crossing Abbey Road, Bob Dylan, Janis Joplin, Jimi Hendrix lighting his guitar on fire. Nearly every iconic photo you can think of from the '60s and '70s were his. He had stories. He always drank a double Knob Creek on the rocks and had Blackbird with dinner upon my recommendation. We became friends. Jim spent time with the great jazz artists too: Miles Davis, Monk, Coltrane. One Wednesday morning before work, I went to his apartment, located just under the pride flag on Castro and Market. It was a small walk-up apartment on the bottom floor. He wasn't feeling well that day, so he was laid out on the couch. The curtains were drawn. On the floor were hundreds of photos. I sat on the dingy brown carpet for hours and looked at photos as he told me stories of the people in them. There were wildly famous photos in the mix. Almost all of them were black and white. He told me about the people in them, who they *were* rather than how they presented themselves to the world. The photos I gravitated toward were raw ones. Jim had an ability to capture the humanity in people. People like Miles Davis and John Coltrane in their most vulnerable states. You can see the suffering in them that created such immeasurable talent. I ended up with three photos that day: one of Coltrane gazing off in the distance, one of Johnny Cash at Folsom prison, and the only color one I saw, Thelonious Monk at the piano in Japan in 1963. I don't put a lot of value on things, but they are some of my most treasured possessions, mostly because they remind me of that day with Jim.

My next stop was Michelin, which is a big deal when you devote your professional life to the service of others. Attaining any recognition is a wild accomplishment. My first Michelin-starred restaurant was a place that made me light up. In retrospect, it also filled so many voids inside of me, giving me a false sense of security and belonging.

Restaurants are composed of the most beautifully broken people on the planet, me included. It takes a special soul to not only want to work eighty hours a week but also to do so with grace. When you begin to hear people's stories, at the highest levels, it becomes clear that the restaurant acts as an escape, as a place to draw much needed comfort and connection. When you take it to the next level and are striving for Michelin stars, uniting with a team around a common goal makes everything else fade away. You spend holidays together, weekends of course, birthdays and anniversaries. You don't request time off; that would be perceived as weakness.

I loved that place more than I loved some members of my family. After a few months as a sommelier, they promoted me to lead sommelier, which meant I was in charge of the massive wine program. When you are working toward something big, you sacrifice all else in pursuit of the goal. We were aiming for a Michelin Star and a Grand Award from *Wine Spectator* at the exact same time. The wine program consisted of 2,700 selections or a half a million dollars in inventory. We built the cellar, literally, from 1,500 to 2,700 nearly overnight. It was a tremendous undertaking, but I was all in.

A Grand Award is one of the highest accolades you can receive in the world of wine. You must have vintage verticals from each producer represented along with a range of vineyards and styles, a huge collection, and massive attention to detail. Your program must be well thought out, organized, and precise. There is a lot of ego involved in the pursuit. There has to be in order for you to willingly choose to sacrifice so much for the cause. While ego plays a part, there is also something incredibly unifying about uniting around a common goal. After years of working in mediocre, poorly run restaurants, landing in this place felt like a dream. The team was cohesive and technically brilliant from a service standpoint. The partners were West Coast Danny Meyer types who preached hospitality and service at every opportunity and were incredibly proficient in business. I was equally as excited as I was intimidated. I was twenty-six years old. There were tenured waiters there that

I feared knew more than me and would dismiss me and my
authority at any opportunity, given the chance. I delved even
harder into my studies simply to quiet the internal critic that held
a megaphone through most of my life. The reality is that I am
a closet introvert who is wildly introspective and quick to judge
myself for the smallest missteps. I have also found myself to be
the authority figure in the room long before I felt like I had any
business being there. The mask was more than a mask at this point
in my life; it was my complete identity. I didn't have a life outside of
the restaurant. I didn't have any hobbies. I was a sommelier who
only had her eye on the top.

Megan and I met on the dining room floor of this Michelin
restaurant. She was the assistant general manager. We realized
early on that even though her mother is Armenian and mine
is from Louisiana, they are, in fact, the same person. Megs is
someone who *shows up*. Full stop. She doesn't wait to see what
you need. She jumps in and gets it done. She's a Virgo, meaning
she is a taskmaster and a list maker. She considers plan A-Z
when doing anything and is fully prepared if anything goes awry.
She is someone you want in the trenches with you. She became
my sister-friend.

When we got our Michelin star, it was wildly validating. It
brought us together in a way I had never experienced. We were
no longer divided by our positions, roles, or titles; we were one
unit that had just achieved something extraordinary. The entire
crew went out onto Sacramento Street. I sabered champagne; we
hugged and cried. That same night, the juxtapositions of my life
came loudly into focus.

The night we got our first star, I was on the dining room
floor when the manager told me that there was someone on
the kitchen phone for me. I immediately knew something had
happened to my father. Sean was on the phone, panic in his voice.
He had gone to dinner with my folks, and my dad collapsed.

"It's bad," he said. I was able to leave service early that night to
run to the hospital. When I arrived, my dad was sitting in a hospital
bed smiling.

"They think I had a stroke, but I'm fine. Ready to get out of here." This high and low was such a physical representation of my life's story. The level of caregiving that was happening both in my personal and professional life became a cornerstone.

Now that I have had a longer lens with which to view my upbringing and early childhood, the fear of the bottom falling out became a bit of a theme for me. The bottom did fall out the day my dad was diagnosed with cancer. It set the stage for the continuous back and forth to hospitals, wondering what I would see when I arrived. What I didn't learn until later was that even when everything turns out okay, your body only knows the fear, tightness, restriction, and the fight-or-flight response that comes when you are confronted with the unknown time and time again. Even when your mind is certain that everything is okay, your body still holds onto that fear, which can become so deeply ingrained that it becomes a part of you, the place you act and think from, rather than a one-off experience.

The quest for a Grand Award required a massive build-out that I did with my boss at the time. He and I had an interesting relationship. He is type A and actually reminds me a bit of my father, so I knew both how to survive with him and how to push his buttons. I was immature and got a bit of a kick out of driving him nuts. I learned a lot from him, although I was too immature to admit it at the time. The best lesson was my final year.

He knew how ingrained I was in the everyday happenings of the restaurant, so he sat me down and said, "This year, you will be judged by how well the restaurant runs in your ABSENCE." It was time to learn how to delegate, how to manage others, how to let go. It was a wildly challenging lesson met with frustration at every corner. Turns out, you grow when things are hard. When I put in my notice, I walked into his office with tears streaming down my face. He looked up from his computer and said, "Well, you're either quitting or you're pregnant." I wasn't pregnant. I had hit the glass ceiling. I wanted to take on more responsibility. I wanted to grow, but there was nowhere for me to go.

When I was younger, I attached so much of my happiness to the achievement of the goal rather than being obsessed with the process. The folks that stay in restaurants at the highest level, and receive the recognition they deserve, are the ones that have one eye on attaining the goal while being absolutely obsessed with the process, with the day to day. Even three-star Michelin restaurants can be rather thankless jobs. Achieving a James Beard award, or a Grand Award, or another star is simply a way to bring validation to the work that is done day in and day out, which requires dedication and consistency that is unparalleled.

Restaurants are sacred spaces where communities are built. They are businesses that sell feelings and experiences through the lens of food and wine. They are places where people are cared for at the deepest level. I know for many that food is just something to consume when you're hungry, but for me, restaurants are the core of all that is good. While these establishments literally sell food and wine, what they really sell is pure human connection rooted in authenticity. The butterfly effect restaurants have is profound. From vendors to staff to guests, the web of connection is vast and unending. I could write an entire book about the beautiful souls that I've had the good fortune to meet in this space and in this way. It is the people, that connective energy, that kept me coming back year after year, showing up each day, in the hope that my words and actions would benefit others in a meaningful way.

Crawfish (or Shrimp) Étouffée

This is also my mom's recipe. Mitch Rosenthal, detailed in this chapter, worked for the iconic Paul Prudomme in New Orleans. This dish will always remind me of him and Town Hall.

Wine Pairing: Hermitage Blanc or Crozes-Hermitage Blanc

Ingredients

Seasoning Mix
2 tsp salt
2 tsp ground red pepper (cayenne)
1 tsp white pepper
1 tsp black pepper
1 tsp dried sweet basil
½ tsp dried thyme

¼ cup chopped white onion
¼ cup chopped celery
¼ cup chopped green bell pepper
7 tbsp vegetable oil
¾ cup all purpose flour
3 cups stock
2 sticks unsalted butter
2 lbs peeled crawfish tails or
    medium shrimp
1 cup finely chopped green onion
4 cups cooked rice

Instructions

1. Mix the seasoning mix.

2. In a cast-iron skillet over high heat, heat the oil until it begins to smoke, then add the flour and whisk to make the roux, cook 3-5 minutes or until golden brown.

3. Remove from heat and stir in the Holy Trinity (minced onion, celery, bell pepper) plus 1 tbsp of the seasoning mix. Sauté for about 5 minutes.

4. In a saucepan, bring 2 cups of stock to a boil, gradually add the roux, and whisk until it is fully dissolved.

5. In a larger sauce pan, melt 1 stick of butter and stir in the crawfish (or shrimp).

6. Add the other stick of butter and 1 cup of stock plus the seasoning to taste. Cook until reduced into a thick sauce.

7. Serve over rice.

CHAPTER 5

Breaking the Place Setting of Identity

I landed at Stock & Bones in 2012. They had five restaurants spread across three cities and two states. I was the beverage director for all. In my previous role, I was so involved with the day to day and the minor details that were mandatory in order for the machine as a whole to function. In this new position, more responsibility oddly meant more freedom. I was no longer scheduled for shifts but was a floater and would move from place to place. Coming from such a tight restaurant to this structure was unexpectedly isolating. I also thought my path would lead me to more Michelin restaurants. I wanted to run the beverage program at a famous restaurant like The French Laundry. I idolized those roles and considered them the best positions in the business. I had set my sights high and was still being driven by ego, but the reality was that I also wanted to be a mother. I knew that this new role and increased flexibility were the only ways to make that dream a reality, yet I found myself unexpectedly angry about the transition. I felt like it was not my choice, like I had been handed this new role, which I was proud of, but it felt like I was somehow stepping in the wrong direction. That transition made me resentful. In retrospect, when the ego clings to the identities we've created for ourselves, we are bound to feel some friction.

The company was owned by Doug Washington and two brothers, Steven and Mitchell Rosenthal, and was run by some of the most kick-ass women I have met to date. All of the highest leadership positions were held by women. These ladies could run circles around the men I had worked with, and they were FUN. There were always shenanigans to get into. My lack of rebellion up until that point, being the "good girl," had hit a critical mass. My father's illness had made me steadfast in my will to succeed up to that point. The move to this new role, and the isolation I felt there, made me want to rebel, to burn it all to the ground. I spent my first few years with them getting the job done during the day and acting like a rebellious teenager at night. It is not a time in my life that I am particularly proud of; in fact, it laid the groundwork for some massive upheaval down the road, which I take responsibility for my part in creating. It is important to acknowledge the part we play in other people's stories, how our actions affect others, and how, even subtly or subconsciously, we are planting seeds that can germinate and grow later into something desirable or into a shitstorm.

Doug Washington was *the* restaurant guy in San Francisco in the '90s, charming and over the top, and a connector in the deepest sense of the word. You never knew what you were going to get with Doug. He likes to get a rise out of people, to catch you off guard. Being charming and memorable is an art he has mastered. He commands space and seems to float on a dining room floor, deeply connecting with everyone around him. When I first started at Stock and Bones, he asked me what my hobbies were. My long answer was about restaurants and dining and wine and sharing meals. The short answer was that I didn't have any.

"This is the year we find you some hobbies," he would say. He encouraged me to begin to look for some balance in my life. He helped me, early on, to see that there was meant to be a life lived outside of the four walls of a restaurant.

He also taught me about how to connect deeply and efficiently with others, efficient being the operative word. He would waltz into the restaurants on any given night and would connect with every single person from the guests, to the bartender, to the busboy, to the dishwasher the exact same way. He would pause, look deep into their eyes, and speak to them as if there wasn't a single other person in the room. I watched his magic countless times and was always mesmerized by how quickly he could come and go yet how big the mark would be that he would leave. It was an art that I respected a great deal. I began to see through his actions that impact can happen through intentionality rather than time spent. In the restaurant world, as with many careers, we are rewarded for being busy, pushing papers, or logging hours. Doug may have spent less time at the restaurants than any of us, but the impact he had was profound.

Steven and Mitchell are joined at the hip, two brothers from Jersey who are absolute salt-of-the-earth people. They ran the kitchen for Wolfgang Puck at Postrio in the '90s and have since done everything together. They also couldn't be more different if they tried.

Steven and I got along very well from day one. We found common ground through our shared love of the mechanics of running a business. He was the numbers guy, and by that point, I felt confident in my ability to make a business money. He appreciated what I brought to the table. He was also the first person I told that I was pregnant.

"I-am-pregnant-but-I-have-a-plan" came out of my mouth as if it was all one word. He supported me in a bigger way than maybe anyone I have ever worked for. He is introverted and very detail-oriented, which can be a tricky combination for most restaurant people, but to me, he is a treasure and a mensch and someone I am so incredibly grateful to have worked for and to call a friend.

Mitchell is larger than life. He is a love, someone who brings light and energy into every space he is in. Covered from the neck down in tattoos, which he proudly shows off, he is a chef, a cook really, and is still quick to jump onto the line during a busy dinner rush. He knows food intimately and has a wildly refined palate. In 2018, Mitchell was diagnosed with colon cancer. He underwent treatment but didn't miss a day of work. One night, while hovering near the pass, a guest walked by and recognized him.

"Mitchell, wow, you look great!" was met with, "Thanks!! I have ass cancer!" with a giant grin on his face. That is Mitch: joyful, unrestrained, no filter. He requires human connection, thrives around people, and brings so much joy just by being.

This restaurant group was such a tight little community, and a place I felt so incredibly supported. Steven and Mitchell had become like family. They created the safest place for one of the first steps toward cracking that identity I had created: motherhood.

Motherhood is a powerful gift. It changes you at your core. It reroutes your north star. It sabotages ego, forces you to face the deepest, darkest parts of yourself only in an effort to be better for them. No one tells you that every decision you make as soon as you become a mother is no longer about you but about what is best for the greater good. Not as a martyr, but as someone who is holding the responsibility of someone else's childhood in your hands.

Hunter was born after a grueling thirty-six hours of back labor. The delivery was not according to my birth plan, not even close, but when they put that baby on my chest and he looked at me, I felt like I had known him my entire life, like this wasn't the first time we had done this. I noticed a deep dimple on his left cheek and these incredibly soulful eyes. He was soft and sweet, and a connector from the moment he arrived. We named him Hunter Thelonious, after Thelonious Monk, the iconic jazz pianist from the 1960s.

When I left on maternity leave, I was terrified. How in the world could I spend twelve weeks not working? Work was my identity, my purpose, my everything. I didn't have hobbies or interests outside of restaurants, food, and wine. I told everyone as I left, just thirty hours before I went into labor, "I'm sure I will be back sooner." No one in my circle, which at that point mostly included the people I worked with, had kids. I was the first. The first days with Hunter were magical. I was shocked that I could just stare at him sleeping all day. I didn't need music or TV or podcasts, just him and me, in bed snuggled up. As the date approached where it was time to go back to work, my sweet little boy stopped taking a bottle. My mom tried, my mother-in-law tried, all to no avail. He would go on a hunger strike if it wasn't me. I was devastated.

I called Steven, choking back tears and said, "I can't do it. I can't leave him. I don't know what to do."

Steven's reply was on brand, short, sweet, and wildly unexpected, "So bring him."

"Bring him where? To work?"

"Yeah, why not?"

I had no clue how we would do it, but when we went back to work, we went together. I had become a different person in those short twelve weeks, and I had an outward attachment, in the form of a cute human child, to show the world that I was forever changed.

One day, we had a chef's meeting with just me, the owners, and the chef team from one of the restaurants, all of which were men. Hunter got fussy, so I offered him a boob. If you know anything about tiny people, when you feed them, they will often simultaneously have a blow-out. There I was, boobs leaking, with my tiny baby with shit all the way up his back to his neck, trying to add value to the conversation. I got down on the floor with baby H, stripped him butt naked, one ear on their conversation, trying to poke my head up to drop nuggets of wisdom. Up until that moment, what I told myself and the world was, "Sure, being a woman is different; you just have to work harder." That scene painted a wildly different picture, one where I learned in an instant how different being a woman was.

We are sold the narrative that women can do it all. Often to do so, we must leave our babies, our nurturing side at the door to succeed in a masculine world. I don't know a world that is more androcentric than that of fine dining restaurants. Even still, it's the women who tend to take the least amount of shit. Having a baby in restaurants was usually deemed a death sentence for your career. The "she'll be back" always met with "we'll see." More often than not, she (whoever she was) didn't come back. Strapping a baby to my chest in this environment was an outward expression of what I have termed my "only child syndrome," which is simply my core belief that I can do anything all by myself. I have learned countless times that I can't, that it's futile, yet I often find myself in this precarious predicament. Balancing restaurant work and motherhood was wild. I used to say that restaurants prepare you for a newborn because you are accustomed to working long hours, being high functioning after little to no sleep, and getting yelled at for no apparent reason, but it was *tough*. The physical toll I could handle, but the emotional toll was unexpectedly painful. When I did leave Hunter, I felt like my entire body was on fire. I pushed through it for no other reason than a deep-seated need to prove myself.

We eventually got the hang of it and settled into a new routine as a unit of three. Just a couple of months after Hunter turned one, I found out I was pregnant with Miles, whom we named after Miles Davis. Miles was ten days late and pushing ten pounds. After a slightly traumatizing birth with Hunter, I was committed to having an unmedicated birth. Medical interventions, while often necessary, felt to me like relinquishing control. My sweet cousin says it perfectly: "There is a secret in our culture, and it's not that birth is painful; it's that women are strong." Miles gave me the incredible gift of knowing my power. I didn't know how strong I was until that day. Just by arriving, he made me feel like I could do anything.

Becoming a mother was simultaneously beautiful and wildly unsettling. I didn't know myself outside of my work. Motherhood forced me to remove some of the identity of "sommelier" to make room for "mother." Motherhood would become the north star for how I would grow and build my business. Being present for my boys, not chasing egocentric goals, but rather living a life of presence and balance in the midst of the busy have become my core principles. Becoming a mother was the first step in cracking me open to reveal my true authenticity. There is incredible power in femininity, in nurturing, in motherhood.

Early on, motherhood felt like a hindrance, like it would in some way hold me back. I began to truly understand that we live in a masculine world but had not yet realized that femininity is a superpower. Mothers are the ultimate creators. I was still trying to mask, to be the person I was before children, which in retrospect caused a tremendous amount of suffering.

Becoming a mother also made me realize that building a life outside of the four walls of a restaurant was imperative. In January of 2020, I stepped out on my own as a restaurant consultant, a fractional beverage director of sorts. I had nine restaurants spread across three states with two more opening that year. Oddly, having more responsibility also meant having more freedom, to work from home, to cook dinner most nights, to raise my boys. Like all of us in the hospitality industry, we had no idea what was coming in a few short months, but the path I was forging lit me up. I was committed to holding the two things I loved most at that time: motherhood and a life in restaurants.

Lamb (or Goat) Chop Lollipops
with Mushroom Risotto

When my boys were little I often made goat or lamb chops, aka "meat with a handle." Easy for toddlers to eat while roaming and delicious for adults as well!

Wine Pairing: Sicilian Red from Etna

Ingredients

1 lb lamb or goat chops
Olive oil
Maldon Salt
Rosemary

Risotto
1 cup acquerello or arborio rice
1 cup white wine

4 cups good stock (see 24-Hour Bolognese recipe in chapter 3 for stock instructions)
1 lb mixed mushrooms
1 white onion
Parmesan cheese
Truffle oil to finish

Instructions

1. Marinate the chops in olive oil, Maldon salt, and rosemary overnight.

2. In a cast-iron skillet, over high heat, brown each side of the chop and cook until desired temperature is reached.

3. Rest the chops before serving.

4. Sauté the mushrooms first, being sure to cook out all of the water, remove from heat, and set aside.

5. Heat the stock in a saucepan so it's warm.

6. Dice the onion and sauté until translucent. Add the rice and stir for a couple of minutes.

7. Add the white wine and let it simmer, then add a cup of stock.

8. Continue to add the stock slowly, stirring all the time. This process takes about 20 minutes.

9. Add the cooked mushrooms once you've reached the desired texture.

10. Finish with a touch of truffle oil, salt, and Parmesan cheese.

CHAPTER 6

Building the Virtual Table in the Midst of Crisis

*People will forget what you said, forget what you did,
but people will never forget how you made them feel.*
—adage frequently attributed to Maya Angelou

When I set out to build my business, I didn't do so with a vision, with a business plan, or with a mission to change the world. I began building my business because restaurants seemed to disappear overnight because of the COVID-19 pandemic. I reacted, propelled by fear and anxiety. What I created filled a massive void for our clients. It also filled a massive void left in me because of the closure of restaurants. I didn't realize it when Acquire was born, but what we were creating would be a gathering place, a virtual table of sorts, rooted in authenticity and human connection. It would be rich. It would connect people across time zones and continents. It would bring purpose and meaning to a profoundly difficult time.

In the spring of 2020, the restaurant industry had a collective identity crisis. I believe there is a common truth across many industries that when you spend your life working, and that work falters, it can be incredibly destabilizing. For many of us in the hospitality industry, we didn't know ourselves outside of our work. We didn't have hobbies or nights or weekends free. We knew intimately how to serve others, how to connect deeply, and how to provide rich experiences for our guests. Subtract the restaurant and the guests, and what are you left with? It is difficult to put into words how massive this loss was. It was a complete displacement of community overnight. I, for one, felt empty. I experienced all of the stages of grief. It felt as if someone in my immediate family had died. I cried, and ran, and did yoga on Zoom, and called to check in on my friends. It was a profound loss and one that we have yet to recover from.

Just a couple of weeks into lockdown, I had a phone call with a woman who ran corporate events. She said she wanted to create a restaurant online, specifically a sommelier experience.

"Of course!" was my reply. *How on earth?* I thought to myself.

In the restaurant world, we often say yes with no clue how we will actually execute. Being scrappy means that we are often called to figure it out. Food and wine belong together, so just offering a wine tasting was off the table. Proudly raised by a Southern woman, and rooted in the belief that feeding people is an act of love, I called my favorite cheese purveyor, Cowgirl Creamery, and my favorite caviar supplier, and created tasting kits comprised of three half-bottles of wine paired with cheese and charcuterie. I sent my new offerings to all of my past customers and clients. I incentivized out-of-work private dining managers from restaurants and gave them a cut of any event opportunity they sent me that booked. I found someone in Napa who could ship alcohol to most states. When I sold my first virtual event, I left my toddlers with my parents, drove to Napa, and learned from the store owner how to ship perishable goods and how to pack the boxes so that the items would arrive in one piece. As we grew, my ship dates became Tuesdays and Thursdays, the only two days my parents took my boys, who had just turned two and four. I would build boxes in the store, pack up a hundred or so boxes, and palletize them to go out.

About a month in, a friend of mine called me with an opportunity to be on NBC's California Live. It was a massive favor. I was still learning the shipping ropes and was nervous to send a package to the producers, worried that it wouldn't arrive in the best condition. I made the decision to drive a tasting kit, along with my two boys, five hours down the 5 south to Los Angeles. This was June of 2020 when we had no clue what we were up against and the world was *scared.* I stayed with a dear friend and her kids for a few days and dropped the tasting kit on the producer's doorway in Northridge on my way back up the 5 to San Francisco. A few days later, she interviewed me live over Zoom. There were little nuggets like this along the way, stepping stones that helped gain exposure and validate what we were doing. We began to grow, mostly by word of mouth.

As we grew, so did the need to hire. Hiring out-of-work restaurant people became my first "why." My community needed a purpose during that staggeringly difficult time. Packing boxes was a far cry from a beautiful restaurant dinner service, but it was something. We were building an internal community.

As we began to gather with guests on Zoom, and the event would wrap up, I would hear people say things like, "This was incredible. This was my only time seeing people this week, and wow, it just feels so good." There was something about sharing the same food and wine experience separated by distance that felt surprisingly human and rich.

My "why" was becoming bigger.

Connection was the cornerstone I long relied upon in restaurants, both internal connection with my team and external connection with guests. We were doing the same thing using Zoom as the medium. We were building a virtual table. The parallels I began to draw from a busy restaurant dinner service to an event on Zoom were also increasing. I could see people light up when they tasted something new. I felt the joy I saw on their faces as they connected with people they hadn't seen in some time. I had never used Zoom prior to the spring of 2020. I never had a reason to. Suddenly, this otherwise sterile tool was becoming a vehicle for connection. In 2020, we scaled to one million dollars in virtual event revenue, hosting events in forty-one different countries and all over the United States.

Gathering in this way, in the virtual space, outside of brick and mortar, led me to create the following mission statement, rooted in the knowing that what we were doing held the power to drive immeasurable connection: "We are a Moveable Feast. The ability to deliver hospitality outside the four walls of a restaurant is limitless."

Acquire was profitable from day one because we didn't hold inventory, and we had next to no labor costs. Our rent was a warehouse space that cost $800 a month. The only product or labor costs that were incurred happened once an event was sold. That event was paid for within thirty days and so was the product and the labor. We didn't have a marketing or a sales team. Everyone simply made a cut of the profit.

No investors required.

This wasn't my first experience getting scrappy to figure out how to make it all work. Bootstrapping felt like the lowest risk path forward. Taking on more inventory or full-time staff all felt increasingly risky, and I was not in a position where I felt like I could take risks.

Outwardly, we were successful. The rush of building something that was working by common metrics was exhilarating. Inwardly, I felt a profound sense of guilt. My community was suffering in a major way. I will never forget the night that Steven called me on March 16th, 2020, just before dinner. He was quiet. We both knew what he was going to say.

"I'm sorry, but I don't think we'll be able to use your consulting services anymore." His throat was tight.

I held back tears. "I totally get it, no worries. Let me know what you need. I love you guys," was all I could get out before we changed the subject to small talk. As soon as I hung up the phone, I went on a run and sobbed. "Run-cries" as I coined them, were commonplace back then. Just a few short weeks after that call, I helped Steven and Mitchell close their businesses. They had both just entered their sixties, a time when you are supposed to be nearing the end of your career. They had spent their lives building a restaurant empire. Suddenly, they were forced to completely start over, a devastating loss. The first few months of the pandemic, I spoke with them daily. I watched as other restaurateurs, my friends, were losing their livelihoods. My former coworkers, who were rarely if ever alone, were being forced into complete isolation. We began donating a percentage of our profits to CORE, a charity that helped restaurant workers in crisis. It was an effort to do something, anything, for others who were suffering. Selfishly, I wanted to quiet the voice in my head, the voice that said that I didn't deserve it and bore the weight of tremendous guilt.

In the early days of Acquire, that voice was loud. It was a mean voice. It usually showed up late at night when I was trying to sleep. It told me I wasn't good enough, that I was projecting a false image. There are tactical things that happen when you start a business: you build a website, do a photoshoot, start a social media strategy. All of these things project the same image of success. This wasn't the first time the critic showed up. It was there on the dining room floor at twenty-four years old as a sommelier. I was wearing a white dress. It was actually the dress that I wore for my high school graduation. I made little to no money in that very prestigious job. A very well-known sommelier came in for dinner. He was the wine director at The French Laundry, a three-star Michelin restaurant that was the best restaurant on the West Coast. I coveted his position and dreamed of holding that title one day. I was *nervous*. He looked at me, down his nose, and said, in his French accent, "Wow, you don't see a sommelier wearing white every day." Immediately, I was a rookie. I had no place being there. I was less than. That inner critic carried a megaphone in my head for most of my life.

As I've grown older, I have learned to sit with that critic, to ask her what she means when she says the things she says. Often the critic is a guide that can help us to become the best versions of ourselves. She hasn't been around for a while, mostly because I finally feel like I am stepping into my true self, who I was always meant to be. When I started to write this book, she showed herself again, loud and clear.

"Who do you think you are? You haven't done *anything*. It's not like you're Sara Blakely. Who would care about what you have to say?"

Today, I realize that the critic arrives when we are doing what we should be doing, when we are pushing ourselves outside of our comfort zone and into a place we, perhaps, don't feel we belong. Just because the voice of self-doubt is loud doesn't mean that

it is correct. The critic comes from a place of fear, but also exists
to protect us from the things that might hurt us. The reality is
that when you are growing and pushing yourself outside of your
comfort zone, you might fail. You might stumble upon things that
hurt you. But that doesn't mean you shouldn't do it. It actually
means you *should*.

When we began hosting virtual events on Zoom, it was a time
that was fraught with fear and isolation. We were "together" on
a screen because we couldn't be together in real life. It was a
Band-Aid, a stopgap, a way for our clients to continue to connect
with their clients, prospects, and team members in a creative,
but not preferred, way. It was clear that people got over it rather
quickly. I think when you're forced into something, it can be really
difficult to see the beauty in it. Zoom is in no way a replacement for
gathering in person. During 2020 and 2021, it was the only option.
That time, for me, was a moment where I saw humanity in its truest
form. We got to know each other in such a deep way because we
were in each other's homes. We met each other's kids, pets, and
partners. So much of that time was messy. Sharing our mess, our
authenticity, was what allowed us to connect deeply. For someone
who spent my career reading people in restaurants, Zoom gave me
a further lens for understanding who people truly were.

In the fall of 2020, when Acquire began to really take off, Megan,
from that first Michelin restaurant, was my first phone call: "Help
me create the structure, then help me hire someone to do it. That's
it; that's all I need."

We dove headfirst into what came next in the winter of 2020. It
was *wild* and fun and a little chaotic. I asked her to be my business
partner at the end of that year because she was like the other half
of me, the organized half that read fine print. She stood by my
side through the most difficult times. Acquire simply would not be
what it is without her.

In December of 2020, we hosted a local venture capital firm for
their holiday party. Our chef, who had previously worked as the
chef de cuisine at Spruce and had spent eight years at The French
Laundry, prepared 175 four-course meals. We hand-delivered kits

to all of their homes, complete with wine pairings, cheese and charcuterie boards, glassware, and gifts. We met online and shared a meal. We also watched as 131 of their children built and decorated Christmas cookie trees on another Zoom link with our pastry chef.

December of 2020 was a particularly rough time for the hospitality industry. The holidays are typically crazy busy. We spend our lives creating memorable moments for others. On any given night in December, prior to 2020, you would find me on a dining room floor, "Santa Baby" blaring for the nine thousandth time, pouring wine, greeting guests. At this point, San Francisco was a ghost town, filled with shuttered restaurants. It felt like a graveyard.

At the end of this insane event we hosted, I thanked them through tears: "Thank you for giving us purpose, for allowing me to hire out-of-work restaurant friends, to build tasting kits in my driveway, which in turn built a community. Thank you for giving us the opportunity to create moments filled with love and intention at a time when we are being asked to stay isolated."

My perspective on the power of Zoom to create rich connections shifted even more dramatically that night.

* * *

The reality is that all of our parts show up at the table: the confident, the insecure, the critic, the tenacious. I used to say that in the spring of 2020, "I got lucky." The thing I created worked. "I got lucky" is something I hear a lot of successful people say, women especially. I do believe that the Universe helps us when we are on the right path, but it is more than luck. Luck downplays the effort and the work that it took to get where we are. Luck might have played a part, but so did failure, resilience, decision-making, and all of the other parts. Luck takes the credit from the people who are working hard toward a goal and puts it out into the world. It says that the achievement was something else's doing, not our own. It is an easy way to not sound boastful or prideful, but "I got lucky" doesn't tell the entire story. If you had an idea and you ran with it, despite having no clue whether or not it would succeed, then you started with courage, not luck. If, like me, you were shoved out of your comfort zone and given no choice in the matter, you didn't get lucky. You persevered in the face of hardship.

Initially, we created something, and it worked. One event would turn into four. We were all word of mouth, fielding inbound calls and emails for events.

It was reactionary.

I was grieving the loss of restaurants, and rather than feel those feelings, I started a business. That business made me so busy that I, once again, kicked a lot of healing down the road. We hired more people and utilized our sommelier friends as event hosts. We began hosting chef-driven experiences and offering gifting, but virtual events were still our primary source of revenue. We leaned into our Michelin-starred background and began to see that hospitality was our clear differentiating factor.

When I stepped into the world of corporate events, I honestly found it to be a bit sterile. It amazed me how much time people spend together at conferences, at meetings, or social gatherings that often feel void of connection.

People just want to feel something.

I knew early on that hospitality would be our cornerstone. Injecting hospitality into this space became another "why." Hospitality is all about how we show up for one another. It is going out of your way for someone else for no other reason than you care about how you make others feel. It is the opposite of transactional.

It is rich. It is human.

Hospitality became our secret weapon for bringing humanity into the way we do business and for cutting through the noise in a sea of events. We spend so much of our lives working that meeting each other with grace, compassion, and genuine connection is the quickest way to bring meaning to our work.

The pandemic was a wild time for those of us in the restaurant business. We all just wanted to go back to work in restaurants, but we had also tasted freedom. We saw sunsets, which might sound strange, but dusk was a time I always spent indoors, serving dinner. I even felt a little naughty, reminiscent of cutting school as a kid, when I would be "in the world" and not in a restaurant at sunset. One of my restaurant friends got an RV and drove around the US working as a campground host. We were raising our own children, some of us for the first time.

Two things can be true at the same time: You can love something so deeply that you don't know where you end and it begins, AND you can want to create a life of balance that fits your overarching needs, allowing you more flexibility and freedom.

During this period of time, Sean and I had a beautiful life. We had moved to a suburb outside of San Francisco with a big backyard and a pool. I spent most mornings with my two littles out on the Slip 'N Slide in the yard. We would bake and build forts and Legos. Miles, my youngest, has a very busy mind, so I would set up stations for him. I would get on my computer, and he would move from one activity to the next, occasionally stopping to ask me for something. Hunter, my sweet, very mellow, older son, would usually watch cartoons. Sean worked from a downstairs office. My space was feral and messy and loud, but I liked it that way. It reminded me of restaurants, which I was desperately missing. Each night, I would cook a nice dinner, and Sean and I would sit at the table, drink a bottle of wine (or two), and talk. Regardless of how we are doing we have always connected deeply about what we are working on. That dynamic always felt comfortable. He has always been my biggest mentor. He helped me significantly during the early days of Acquire. He also felt a million miles away. If I am being honest, I couldn't tell if it was my grief about restaurants, my complete isolation, or him; it was all so subtle, but we felt different. I brushed it off as nothing. There was nothing obvious to point a finger at. We were still "good," so why rock the boat? When I did point out how far away he felt, it was dismissed. My attempt to talk to a therapist was met with, "We have the tools to figure it out ourselves," not dissimilar to my mother's take on therapy as "that is what other people do, we don't need that." I complied.

The Perfect Roast Chicken
aka "Trauma Chicken"

If you live near me, and you've experienced anything challenging in your life, you have very likely received a roast chicken on your doorstep. Coined a "trauma chicken," the perfect roast chicken feels like pure comfort and home. We make this once a week in our house and when we travel for long periods and find ourselves missing home.

Wine Pairing: Red Burgundy

Ingredients
1 whole chicken
Maldon salt
Butter
Rosemary
1-2 sweet potatoes
Olive oil

Instructions
1. Rinse the chicken inside and out and pat dry with a paper towel.

2. Place breast side up in a cast-iron skillet and salt the skin.

3. Put butter and rosemary under the skin on each of the chicken breasts, salt with Maldon.

4. Take 1-2 sweet potatoes and dice into cubes. Place them around the chicken in the pan and drizzle with olive oil and salt.

5. Roast in the oven at 425 for 1 hour or until it's an internal temperature of 165 degrees and golden brown.

CHAPTER 7:

Ashes and Woodgrain

I am someone who is radically optimistic by nature. It is still unclear whether or not this is a deep coping mechanism, or who I innately am, but I am quick to give reason to my suffering, to see the positive, the learning lessons, the beauty in all of the heartbreak. Maybe it is the only way to truly face the hard things that happen. Maybe it's the only way to make it out alive. Ram Dass says that if you rid the world of suffering, you rid people of what makes them uniquely them. Our stories, our trials, our "messy," are what makes us uniquely the people that we are today. Each of these experiences is simply walking us toward our authenticity. Suffering comes to us as a gift.

It is easy to look back on the most difficult moments of our lives with gratitude once we have reached a place of balance and equanimity, to say, "this happened *for* me not *to* me" when the work to get to a place of ease has been so focused, so nonlinear, and so much hard work. We can only grow in direct proportion to how willing we are to sit with what is uncomfortable. I heard a very wise person say that a memory without a trigger is wisdom.

I felt that.

Sometimes, we are forced to sit with what is uncomfortable through no choice of our own. In fact, the harder we grasp at the identities we have created for ourselves, the harder we must be shaken to get free.

My business fell apart just as my personal life did. I have come to believe that this is not a coincidence. When Acquire was built the first time, in the spring of 2020, it was reactionary. It was codependent. It was desperate. It worked, meaning we were profitable, we hired people, and we built beautiful connections outwardly, but the structure was unhealthy. The summer of 2021 kicked off the hardest time in my life. The foundation of my world completely shattered. In the fall and winter of 2021, we were still busy. I was completely out of my body, but I still had to work. This modus operandi was one that I was very familiar with. Mask up, put on the show, be the person everyone is expecting you to be was a look I had mastered.

This time, it was harder.

Marriage is a wild contract we enter into. "I will love you until I die," typically when we are far too young to truly understand the weight of that commitment. We are a thousand people in every lifetime. If we're doing it right, we grow, we change, we evolve. The person you marry at twenty-five is not the same person at twenty-eight, let alone sixty. Often, when the foundations we lay in the beginning are not set up to withstand the test of time and stress and anger and resentment, we are given a gift that breaks it open, exposing all of the flaws, giving us the opportunity to put it back together in a way that actually works for the long haul. We must allow things to get messy, to break them apart in order to put them together better, stronger.

Sean is a gentle soul and someone I feel immensely safe with. He is a nurturer. He has a gift for connection and sees people on a soul-level. He is the deepest feeler I know, which is likely what drew me to him, like a magnet, all those years ago. We were devoted to each other from day one in a way that felt concrete and unshakable. Never once, in all of our years, did I consider that something like this would happen to us.

Infidelity is wild because of the way it distorts the truth of everything around you. If this could be true, what else is a lie? It is incredibly disorienting. Let me preface this by saying that this part of my story is not unusual. In fact, most people who are in long-term, committed relationships experience infidelity in some form or another; they just don't talk about it. I also have become crystal clear on the part that I played in this unraveling. The foundation for what happened to us was laid so many years before the ground we stood on opened up beneath us. When I chose to forgo the path of chasing Michelin stars, the seed of resentment was planted. Sean became the physical manifestation of my responsibilities rather than my partner. He wanted me home and around more. Instead of being grateful for having a partner who wanted to be with me, I resented him for it. Resentment might be one of the most destructive forces in a relationship. It can take years to develop into a disruption, yet it is always there, steeping under the surface, causing tension and frustration. Resentment and anger are our bodies' worst enemies. Together, they kill peace. Resentment can come up so easily as we get older and take on the responsibilities of caring for children, aging parents, and partners. I didn't face my anger or resentment, so it reared its ugly head in the most disruptive of ways.

When the truth came out, and the shock subsided, we went to our separate corners. Sean went to the guest room downstairs while I stayed in the master. In all reality, I tried to run. I think it's common when things like this happen: to try to get as far away as possible, to protect ourselves from further hurt. Staying put and facing the enormity of what happened is tougher in a lot of ways. Divorce was still the only option in my mind, the only way I knew how to stand up for myself. We 'nested' and lived separate lives while remaining under the same roof. It was a complicated time that was layered with isolation and grief. Our boys always came first. How we wanted them to feel through all of this was as our north star. We refused to shatter their lives simply because we had shattered ours. We began to work on ourselves as individuals for the first time, taking on every modality available to us: talk therapy, energy healing, yoga, acupuncture, you name it. I coined it "the saddest wellness retreat of all time." Today, I am immensely grateful for the privilege to have had access to all of those tools, these guiding forces that acted as guardrails as we unraveled and then put ourselves back together, first as individuals and eventually as a couple. To this day, our boys don't know we are divorced, not many people do, actually. Probably because we are currently living the most magical and rich version of our relationship to date.

The reality is that my boys will face countless things in life that will shake them at their core. Keeping them in the dark about what has made us who we are today is not protecting them from that truth. The day will certainly come, long before they read these words, when we will tell them our story, a story of triumph and work and commitment, not of pain, shame, suffering, or victimhood. Our relationship today sits outside of marriage, but it is stronger than it has ever been. It's taken all this disruption to see him, to see us, with clarity and to know that the feeling we had, all those years ago, of coming home, was not because of the holes we were looking to fill, but were because of something deeper, something profoundly unknown. That inclination that we've done this before, a resounding YES, to partnership, to our future, whatever it holds, to **unconditional** love.

We wanted to keep the divorce neat and tidy, so we shared a lawyer. Our mediation meeting went so well and was so quick and easy, I joked that we should probably just stay married. I don't think our attorney knew what to do with us. The day we signed our papers, we cried and hugged and went out to dinner. We needed to grieve the loss of our marriage, and even though we were still worlds apart, we leaned on each other to do so. This deeply sad moment in our lives, of course, involved a restaurant. Snail Bar is this sweet space in Oakland that sparks joy for both of us. The chef worked in Spain and is immensely talented. They serve natural wine. It feels a lot like our favorite places in Paris. We sat on the sidewalk and ate and talked. When we got home, we went to our separate rooms. We didn't know it then, but the coming back together began the minute we metaphorically lit our marriage certificate on fire. We needed to break down the construct in order to build it back better.

In September of 2021, just two months into our new arrangement and still heavily in the midst of the pandemic, I flew to France alone. It was my first trip without my kids. I worked harvest at one of my favorite wineries: Mas de Daumas Gassac, just outside of Montpellier. I picked grapes and worked in the cellar, shoveling tanks. I spent a lot of time alone and in nature. There was something so healing about that trip, a reminder of why I got into wine in the first place, balanced by a realization of just how strong I am, on my own two feet, without the identity of mother, sommelier, or wife. It was really hard being away from my boys, but that forced space is something that I am profoundly grateful for.

After being in Southern France for a few days, I took the train up to Paris. I met a tattoo artist at a wine bar, a young guy from Argentina that was well known for creating really delicate pieces with absurdly fine lines. After a day trip to Champagne, I went straight from the Gare de Lyon to his tattoo shop. A bottle of natural wine and a lengthy discussion later, he drew a beautiful small piece that was to go on the inside of my right wrist. It is a perfect oval-shaped wreath with one side darkened and the other side light. The wreath represents divine feminine energy and the process of going through the darkness to step into the light. After this trip, I felt empowered. I understood my strength. I wanted a literal symbol of that feeling. I wanted it placed where I could see it, a constant reminder of my own power, of the need to experience the darkness in order to appreciate the light.

When I got home, my house still felt heavy. The air was thick for some time, filled with sadness and weight. Sean and I spoke openly during couples therapy, but mostly avoided each other in the space in between. One morning, I woke early to find him in the kitchen. We began a lengthy conversation that would uncover some truths I didn't know before. He told me he was depressed, more than depressed really. Broken. My heart split in two again that morning. Only this time, it opened up in a way that I didn't see coming. I saw him, for the first time, in his true authenticity. I was dumbstruck by how I could have missed it for so long. This didn't excuse his behavior, but it made me understand. When you are at your lowest of lows, it becomes so much easier to get lost in fantasy, to not fully grasp the repercussions of your actions, to not really care. My heart broke again, this time for his pain, for his quiet suffering.

When your heart breaks, you can choose to armor up and become angry and defensive, or you can choose to leave your heart open. Truly seeing him for the first time made me feel all of it all at once. Empathy is about being with the experience of another. It is feeling what others feel. It is grieving when they grieve. I forgave him before that moment, but up until that point, I didn't understand how or why. That moment, at 5 a.m., standing in our kitchen, I understood. I saw him at his lowest point, and I chose to love him unconditionally. Being in partnership, which stands outside of marriage, is seeing all of the flaws and shortcomings, and choosing love and openness over fear and resentment, without hesitation, every single time.

Don't get me wrong—coming back together still took an extremely long time. My bedroom, which felt like a gaping hole when Sean first moved downstairs, had become my safe space. I knew I was healing parts of myself that had been left untouched once I began enjoying my solo time and a space to call my own. My big bed felt like it was meant just for me—and the occasional four-year-old who often found his way in there.

Running from my pain, in the winter of 2021/22, also involved a lot of skiing. I feel at ease in the mountains, lighter somehow. In January of 2022, I had a solo day trip to Tahoe planned. I was hesitant to go that morning because I felt wildly anxious the night before. Despite my lack of sleep, I left at 6 a.m. and arrived on the hill as the lifts opened. It was just like any other day. I was coming down a run I had taken countless times before, but this time was going way too fast. As I merged onto a cat track, I didn't see a drop in the run. It was only a couple of feet, but when you're going over forty miles per hour, it's easy to lose your footing.

I fell hard.

My bindings didn't release, so when I hit my head, I slid backward, pulling my legs parallel uphill to stop me. "Check your body" is something I said often to my kids at that point in life, so that phrase echoed in my head. *I'm good. I think I'm good.* I stood up only to find that my left knee felt completely wobbly and disconnected. *I can ski down on one ski,* I thought, but then the nausea came, and it suddenly got dark. I didn't pass out, but my body was telling me that something was really wrong. I looked uphill just as the lights came back on and saw a ski patrol. "It's my knee," I said, and he called for a sled. Turns out, he had graduated from my high school twenty years before me. We laughed, and he said that the ride down would be fast but uncomfortable. As we pulled into the medical area, it dawned on me: I won't be able to run, or move, or do yoga. The tears came full force. I was in zero physical pain, but the thought of having to sit with my internal pain, to not be physically able to move it out, was too much to bear. A torn ACL put me into surgery just two weeks later.

It also put me back in my body.

At that point, Sean and I were little more than two ships in the night. We didn't sit at the table anymore. We didn't eat together. Gathering together in that sacred way made me too sad. It felt too heavy. So we skipped it for the better part of a year. We would exchange small talk, but that was about it. I drove to the surgery center alone, which was an insane feeling. My mother, a full-time caregiver for my father, couldn't get away. Sean felt so far away that I couldn't impose upon him. Megan, my business partner and dear friend, picked me up from surgery, drove me home, and slept in my bed for four days, giving me meds, shuffling my kids, and taking me to doctor appointments. When she left, I began having to rely upon Sean for things that I needed. I couldn't put weight on my leg for three weeks. Showering involved dumping a pot of hot water over my head while sitting on a shower chair that didn't fit into the actual shower. There was a forced vulnerability to that time period, an openness to asking for and accepting help, that further laid the groundwork for bringing us back together.

In the spring of 2022, the world outside of our home went back to normal, our clients completely abandoned virtual events, and I was given an unwanted pause. It was difficult to not go into panic mode. Acquire, the thing I created was *working,* and then it was dead. In retrospect, the pause was exactly what I needed personally at that moment. Don't get me wrong—it made things exponentially harder. Busying ourselves with work and life is far easier than sitting with ourselves, than looking inward to heal the deepest, darkest parts of ourselves. But sit with myself, I did. I put myself back together just as I began putting my business back together. I didn't realize it at the time, but this unwanted pause was laying the foundation for building back everything, including my business, stronger.

Healing ourselves often requires stillness. It is no coincidence that some of the most successful people on the planet also have a mindfulness practice. For me, this wasn't an intentional choice. It chose me. I learned to find gratitude for the lessons that quickly transpired. Stillness allows us time to process all that is unresolved. It creates space to think, to not rush, or run downhill, but to be with our thoughts. I hosted a virtual event two days after surgery and got on a plane to host an in-person event while still on crutches three weeks later, so the sitting with oneself I am describing was still my version of it. It wasn't a silent meditation retreat by any means, but it was the first step on the pathway to slowing down.

> *Ordinarily I go to the woods alone ...*
> *If you have ever gone to the woods with me,*
> *I must love you very much*
> —Mary Oliver, "How I Go To The Woods"

My healing journey has been far from linear. Gaining awareness into who we are is incredibly eye-opening. It requires discomfort. For someone who is near constantly moving, stillness still is the hardest part for me. In the fall of 2022, I found myself on a yoga retreat in Helena, Montana, in the beginning of my rebuilding panic. Wi-Fi didn't work. There was no cell service. Miles, who was four, got sick with croup just as I was leaving for the airport. I was in the middle of nowhere. My nervous system was on fire. Each morning, we would wake up, be silent, and do morning meditation and two-hour yoga practice in front of a roaring fire before we would go to breakfast and speak for the first time each day. I would hike alone, often in the rain, encountering wildlife and solitude. I talked through my story a lot on that trip because we were there to heal, but that was when it felt like it wasn't fitting anymore, like it was an outfit I was putting on. I was not a victim in this situation. I am not a victim of my life. These experiences are gifts that are here to teach us, to force us to go inward and look deeper. It was an incredible reset, a true unplugging and an opportunity to remove the distractions of the everyday. To remove the busy. I settled in and created real space.

When we are vulnerable and raw, anger and resentment act as the protective mechanisms we think will save us. Anger is two things: the mask of sadness and sadness with nowhere to go. Releasing it all is a fundamental need on the pathway to freedom. Early on, my yoga teacher said that "just because we choose to live with an open heart, does not mean that our hearts will always be broken." Moving in the world with an open heart means being open to people and places and experiences. It means leaning into your authenticity and removing the mask even if there is still fear of rejection. By the end of that week in Montana, I felt an insane sense of peace. I hadn't "figured anything out." I didn't have a moment where it all made sense, but forced inaction was actually the first step on the pathway to freedom from my own pain and suffering.

As I began to come back out into the world post-pause, my tone changed. The way I showed up changed. The voice of the business changed, ever so subtly, too. As I began to rebuild my business, this time from a more healed place, the structure of what I was creating was allowed to rest on a foundation that was solid, that was built for the long haul. Rather than using my business to define my life, I let the goal be to create the life I wanted to live, while allowing the business to support that. A micro-adjustment that meant a world of difference.

Sean and I began to change too. We had a softness for each other that hadn't been there in some time. One year into our new arrangement, we took a family trip to Spain and Iceland. We spent real time together, as a unit of four. We laughed. We had adventures. We shared meals, both those cooked on camp stoves and those enjoyed late over plates of anchovies and glasses of white wine in the plaza as we watched our boys play. Sitting together in this sacred way was familiar but simultaneously entirely new. The more healed versions of us showed up at those tables. We were timid, a bit wary, but testing the waters. Gathering in this way allowed us to connect with the familiar while discovering parts of each other that had always been hidden in the past. It allowed us to take another small step forward, set in the knowing that what we were building back was worth fighting for.

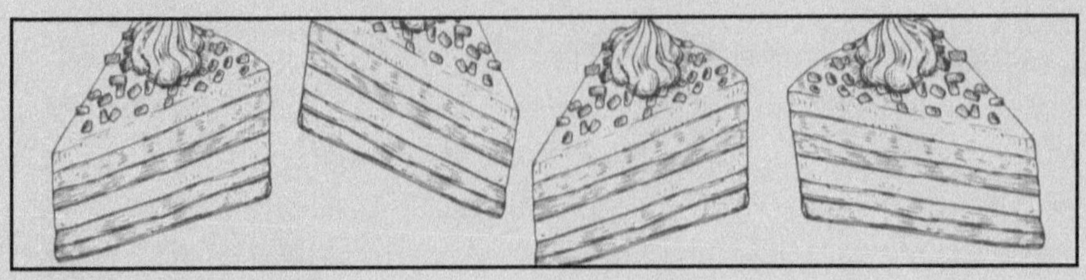

Italian Cream Cake

I am not a baker, but Hunter is. This is the one of the only cakes I have ever made. It was Bertha's recipe as well. If you went to her house, she almost always had one on the counter with a knife in it. My mom has made it over the years, and it's been devoured by friends and family.

Wine Pairing: VEP Chartreuse (because it's delicious)

Ingredients

1 cup buttermilk
1 tsp baking soda
5 eggs
2 sticks unsalted butter
1 tsp vanilla extract
2 cups flour
2 cups sugar
1 cup coconut
1 cup chopped nuts

Icing
1 package cream cheese
1 tsp vanilla extract
1 stick unsalted butter
1 box powdered sugar

Instructions

1. Have all ingredients at room temperature, then mix dry ingredients together.

2. Mix baking soda and buttermilk together and then add slowly to the dry mixture.

3. Bake in three pans at 325 degrees.

4. Mix icing ingredients together and spread between layers and on the top and sides of the cake once cooled.

CHAPTER 8

In the Trenches

We live in a society where we are rewarded for running downhill. The restaurant world runs at a breakneck speed. If you want something done, you do it. There is no job title or role that makes you exempt from the grind. Even the biggest, most grueling projects happen through literal blood, sweat, and tears of everyone on the team. When all of our virtual event clients went back to in-person events in a *major* way, it was devastating. The narrative then was that virtual events were only a thing we did because we couldn't be together. It was yet to become a strategic business choice. Overnight, our business tanked. I quickly found myself grasping at straws, desperate to put my business back together as quickly as possible. In doing so, I created a lot of friction. When we push, literally and figuratively, we are met with resistance, often making it harder for ourselves. When we play an active part in the writing of our stories, while simultaneously allowing things to unfold as they will, we are met with greater ease and peace.

I am a hand-raiser. I still say yes to the things that light me up and run toward them. Perhaps *what* I run toward now has shifted, but the person I am is still wildly predictable in this arena. Much of my recent adult life has been spent trying to find better, more efficient ways of doing the necessary things on our to-do list, so that we can really LIVE our lives in the moments we have on this earth.

One of my favorite feelings is in that space where nervousness meets excitement so closely that it is impossible to tell which emotion is which.

That said, my primary focus today is to not be addicted to
the chaos. Even after we extract ourselves from restaurants, it's
commonplace to create that same fast-paced, high intensity
environment, simply because we feel comfortable there.
Rebuilding from a more healed place meant that what was built
could be rooted in equanimity, rather than chaos. A common
pitfall, one that I fell into, was grasping at what was comfortable,
rather than letting things unfold as they will.

At first I offered too many things. I was a restaurant consultant,
working as a fractional beverage director again for a restaurant
group. We offered corporate gifting and chef-driven experiences.
I sold retail wine to high net worth wine collectors, and we began
helping our clients plan high-impact dinners utilizing restaurants
as the gathering places. We were all over the place.

But I was desperate.

I said yes to everything that equaled revenue even when the
margins were thin. This fear-based response was formed during
my time in restaurants. There was a time when the restaurant
business was more or less printing money. I lived through that time
of excess. I watched year after year as the bottom line dwindled,
despite calculated efforts to reduce costs. I worked for some
insanely skilled operators, and they would even struggle to make
a profit once it was all said and done. Before the pandemic, the
restaurant business was in crisis. It felt desperate and like there was
no way out. I wanted my business to be different.

Rebuilding Acquire, as I rebuilt myself, didn't come without its
roadblocks and challenges. Countless insecurities and trying to
force success laid a roadmap for the undoing, the unlearning that
was required to arrive at a place of trust.

Being reactionary was a default learned from working in
restaurants. In the restaurant world, we are constantly "putting out
fires." Our plans for the day could be derailed because some crisis
has come up that requires our attention. When you operate in this
place day-to-day, your body doesn't know the difference between a
line cook being ten minutes late and the building literally being on
fire. The lightbulb moment came when I realized what power I held

just by taking all of the energy I once used reacting to the drama, and focused it instead on *creating.* Rebuilding my business from a healed place, with that energy, meant building back something set on a solid foundation.

The bottom falling out had also become a bit of a theme for me, so I was operating in a constant state of fight or flight. I felt like I was drowning. I hired consultants, reaching outward toward the external to find anyone who knew more than me to help me navigate how to rebuild my business. When we began to rebuild, I hadn't yet realized the power I held. I hadn't yet learned to trust myself.

I was also often met with not feeling adequately prepared to lead. Being the only kid at the table with grownups felt the same for me as stepping into the world of corporate engagements for the first time. I felt like a fish out of water, underprepared and way over my head. That feeling of insecurity made me look outward for support.

Hiring your weakness is a tactic I wholeheartedly believe in. I know what I am good at, and I know when to stay in my lane. I am not shy about what I don't know. I am certainly not trying to prove anything. I would much rather have a competent team of people who are utilizing their strengths to work toward a common goal than flail about pretending to be good at something I am not.

That said, one of the mistakes I made, more than once, was hiring someone who knew more than me, but then expecting them to do it all. Hiring people that have more experience or know more than you is a wonderful first step on the pathway to growth, but expecting them to do what you need them to do without succinct direction is a pitfall that is easy to fall into. I would often be driven by my own insecurities in these moments. "They know more than me," echoed in my mind. Correct, they may know more than you, which is why they are there, but you are the only one who knows where to steer the ship. Relying upon people for their expertise is a good move, but giving them guardrails is imperative for keeping your business moving in the right direction.

I also hired people I liked, which is something I still do, but without asking the right questions to determine if they were truly a good fit for our small but mighty team. Interviewing can be *tough,* even for someone who declares themself a great read of people. Some people interview so well that you fall in love with the *idea* of what they will bring to the table. Once they're in the door, it can quickly become an entirely different story. I learned, through a series of bad hires, that the moment it feels like it's not working, cut bait. Don't let emotions get involved. I am also a full believer that all bad hires are here to teach us something. Pausing, reflecting inward, analyzing how and why this person ended up a part of the team in the first place, and the part that I played in it was paramount in not repeating the same mistakes. Nothing comes to us by accident, so always look for the lessons.

Unlearning an ingrained communication style also became a priority. The way we communicate on a dining room floor during a busy restaurant service is short, almost curt. When I am overwhelmed, this is my default mode, which is highly out of character. It is simply a language I have learned to mean "let's get it done." What I have realized is that, "let's get it done" is not what people hear. They hear frustration and disappointment, which is never my intention. We also take the mechanics of what we are doing so seriously in restaurants. I remember feeling like my body was on fire when someone would use the wrong hand to drop a plate. That seems absurd to me now, but I have also realized that small errors can have the same effect on my nervous system, and my body doesn't know the difference. Taking a pause before reacting has become a fundamental step in making me the leader I want to be for my team.

The reality is that owning a business is often about getting knocked down over and over again and making the conscious choice to stand back up and work toward your goals. It is being told "no" more than being told "yes." It is choosing to fight for what you believe in, even when the world is telling you it will never work. I often think that entrepreneurship is just resilience masked in confidence. From the outside, it can look like we are still chasing something, still striving for that outwardly defined success. The true intention is to build something meaningful that meets our human need to connect deeply while building lives we don't need to escape from.

Miso-Ginger Marinated Black Cod with Brown Rice and Kale

This dish is light and easy and healthy. A quick go-to for a weeknight. Fish does not need to be marinated for long.

Wine Pairing: Savoie Blanc

Ingredients

4 filets of black cod
1 green onion sliced
3 tbsp soy sauce
¼ cup mirin
¼ cup white miso
2 tsp sesame oil
2 tbsp grated ginger

Sides
Brown rice
Stock (see 24-Hour Bolognese recipe in chapter 3 for stock instructions)'
Olive oil
1 clove garlic minced
1 bunch of kale

Instructions

1. Whisk together the onion, soy sauce, mirin, white miso, sesame oil, and grated ginger. Pour over the cod filets and let marinade for a couple of hours.

2. Pull the fish out and pat dry.

3. Cook over medium high heat in an oiled pan skin side down.

4. Cook the brown rice in stock and sauté the minced garlic in a touch of olive oil.

5. Wash and tear the kale off the stem.

6. Sauté until tender and serve.

CHAPTER 9

Lessons from a Business Rooted in Service

As I rebuilt Acquire, I really fell into what I wanted my life to look and feel like, and then put the business back together to meet that vision, not the other way around. It took a long time and a ton of spiritual work to arrive at a place of trust. Trust that regardless of whether we succeed or fail, it is all for the greater good of our own self-growth and self-discovery. There are lessons in literally every success and every failure. Even in those moments when it feels like you're stuck and there is no pathway forward, you are actively learning lessons that will serve you later in your journey.

It is also okay to not have all the answers. Alua Arthur, in her book *Briefly, Perfectly Human*, says that the "not knowing is where the juice lies." Her words remind me that when we think we have all the answers, we are actually the most stagnant, the least malleable, and the least open to the infinite number of possibilities available to us. Not knowing means we are rife with possibility.

In the spiritual world, we talk about manifestation. In the corporate world, we call it materialization. "How do we materialize our goals?" is corporate speak for "how do we turn our aspirations into reality?" Writing things down is key. Believing wholeheartedly in what you are doing as if it has already happened is imperative. Maybe there is some hubris in entrepreneurship, but you must have absolute certainty that what you are doing will work, and you must believe in it like it already has.

You must be so certain that there is no room for hope.

Let me explain. Hope leaves room for doubt. When you say, "I hope it works," you're expressing that there is a part of you that thinks it might not. And when you leave that sliver of doubt, you open yourself up to the possibility of failure. Hope, while often seen as a positive, is a wolf in sheep's clothing for an entrepreneur. Even when my business was falling apart, I was certain that it would come back. So certain that it felt, at times, like it already had. Certainty in the outcome removes the desperation, the grasping, the fight or flight nature that can penetrate your life and cloud your judgment.

Waiting and being comfortable just being was one of the greatest challenges of my life.

I had a hunch that virtual events would be back. I love people, truly, with all my heart. I also love my soft clothes. I knew I wasn't alone in this feeling. Our social bandwidth had been tried and tested, and turns out, most of the people who are forced to travel day in and day out in the corporate world either hate it or are running from something. Most of the latter are blissfully unaware, but part of healing yourself makes others' wounds impossible to miss.

Building a life you don't want to escape from became a core tenet at Acquire, and that meant for me too. It took a long time for me to see that saying yes to all revenue streams was a distraction. Feeling desperate for revenue means you will take it all on. The reality is that there are only so many hours in the day. Focusing on what we could scale the quickest and would have the highest impact on our clients became the top priority. Then, I removed all that didn't serve that.

Outgrowing what doesn't fit requires flexibility, looking at each choice from all angles, and strategically choosing the best and most efficient path forward. For us, efficiency also meant scalability. High impact, low lift. Virtual events had yet to become a strategic business choice for the business world, but I remained steadfast in my belief: **Virtual events are radical acts of hospitality.**

For one, I believe that giving people their time and therefore their lives back by not requiring them to board a plane for a meeting is an act of love. From a business perspective, a virtual event is a one-hour engagement, compared to our in-person events that require labor, travel, higher product cost, and countless additional hours. The cost to our clients is often roughly the same with lower cost for us. Throwing all we had at the power of virtual events was a no-brainer.

I also love to travel, not work travel, but rather nitty-gritty see-humanity travel. Showing my boys the world is a top priority. Offering virtual events means that I can host anytime from anywhere. It also means that most of my events happen between 1:00 p.m. and 4:00 p.m. Pacific Time, which gives me the day for work and the evenings for home. Living in restaurants for the first half of my life, I had never imagined a world where I could raise my own children. Picking up my kids from school and cooking dinner every night, tasks many find burdensome, felt like an out-of-reach dream. Having gratitude for the freedom that virtual events give me personally makes me a champion for others. Virtual events have literally changed my life and my trajectory and my kids' lives by default. When I say virtual events give you your life back, I actually mean it.

Building a bigger team was also high on my wish list. When I was in restaurants, we would often complain about labor costs and how hard it was to manage hourly employees. The restaurant world had changed. I was proud of the younger generation for standing up for what they believed in and for not working until they dropped. Turns out, managing people that don't bend over backward at every request is harder than managing people who do. I didn't wish for it to be different but acknowledged how it had changed. As a restaurant management team, we would often joke about where the cause of our aging came from. It certainly wasn't the late-night drinking, but more so the "hourlys." The minute I was out on my own, I craved community with others. The restaurant business is a weird amalgamation of people who have varied pasts but similar needs to fill. The trauma might look different but the results are often the same. Building a team that was not rooted in codependency was one of my first challenges.

It took several lessons and bad hires to get to a place where I knew how to ask the right questions to discover whether or not someone would truly be a good fit. Being crystal clear about what they will contribute and how they will achieve the metrics you set out for them is of utmost importance. First is laying out the mechanics of how you will measure their success. Their success is paramount when it comes to how you *feel* about them being a part of the team. Writing down what will make them successful and mapping a pathway to get there is the best way you can support them to succeed. I also learned that background, experience, and credentials are not a silver bullet. A killer resume and a master's degree is not a guarantee that this person will swoop in and save you. It is up to you to save yourself.

I have also learned to look for people with entrepreneurial spirit who see the whole picture. They understand what they contribute, and when they see a need to fill, they take it upon themselves to fill it. My team today is spread across four states and three time zones. Managing people remotely is new for me. I am learning how to set up the mechanisms so that we can function as a cohesive team. I have also hired people into job functions in which I have no experience, which requires a ton of trust. Growing can also mean letting go. Danny Meyer talks about hiring 51-percenters, or hiring people that care and have strong emotional skills. These are people who, when given a choice, want to go out of their way to do the right thing. People can be trained on the mechanics of *how* you want things done, but you can't train people to care.

In October of 2024, I felt like I had finally honed my hiring skills. I asked a million questions. I took my time. The person I brought on would end up changing the face of my business in a profound way. I had found my footing! And then, just a month later, my dad died. I made time to sit with the grief, but as usual, there was still work to do.

Just as we were setting the stage for 2025, a messaging shift, and what we wanted the business to look and feel like, our marketing lead, an integral part of our team, left without warning. The old me wanted to be frustrated, to get emotional. But the more balanced and healed version simply said, "This is just making space for what needs to come." My new hire literally said, "I don't know what drugs you've done to arrive at that, but I want some." This person leaving did, in fact, kick off a chain reaction that changed the face of my business.

I brought on someone great to run our marketing strategy. We drilled down to who we should be talking to rather than screaming into the void. We began a targeted and calculated approach to acquiring new customers. Field marketers were our target. They had the decision-making power and the budget to pull the trigger without having to go elsewhere for approval.

We heard, time and time again, that our customers were having a hard time driving attendance to their events, so we launched a new offering: go-to-market support. This add-on to our events simply meant that we would take on the heavy lifting for them by targeting their list of prospects and inviting them to our virtual event. This created an "always on" demand-generation strategy for our clients while simultaneously validating our new position as B2B marketers.

In restaurants, we speak about anticipating our guests' needs. Anticipating our clients' needs, being adaptable in what we create to meet those needs is an act of hospitality, just like placing a warm towel with lemon in front of a guest that is just finishing a bowl of mussels. It says, "I noticed you needed this, so I brought it to you before you even had to ask."

I was also lucky to have an amazing business partner, Megan, throughout the first phase of Acquire. Megan and I walked through the trenches together as we both faced gut-wrenching grief in our personal lives at the exact same time. We leaned on each other for far more than work. In June of 2025, Megs took a heart-centered leap into a new career. I felt proud of her, honored that she spent the time she did with me, building this thing I know we both came to love deeply. She leads from the heart and pours herself into her work, which is an impossible characteristic to teach. Her warmth is infectious. She felt irreplaceable, so as she left, I knew that what would come next would be something entirely new.

Back in my grasping-at-straws era, I had tried to hire a salesperson that, in all honesty, we weren't ready for. I made her a generous offer, one I couldn't afford, in hopes that she would be my silver bullet. Luckily for everyone involved, she turned the position down. I didn't know then, but the reason it didn't work out was because I wasn't ready, the business wasn't ready, and the world wasn't yet ready to come back to virtual events. The day Megan left, this person called and said she was ready to take on some part-time work. Again, a low-risk, clear pathway forward to driving revenue. Another validation that even when there is heartbreak in the midst of change, it does clear space for the next thing to come. Allowing ourselves to fully trust this process of doing and undoing is a fundamental part of growth.

Sara Blakely, founder of Spanx, says she asks the Universe for clear signs or guidance when making business decisions. Blakely says that these "signs" are really a metaphor for trusting your intuition for guidance and opening yourself to the greater plan that is unfolding. Many of us have lost touch with our intuition —that guiding voice that tells us where to go or what to do next. This might sound crazy or "woo woo," but I have consistently seen the number 23 throughout my life. It comes at moments when I doubt myself. My kids even see it now and proudly exclaim, "Mom!! Your angel number!" There have been countless times that this number has appeared on my entrepreneurial journey, but there is one way that is so blatantly obvious, it would be tough to miss. When I started Acquire, I built out my profit and loss statements to mirror those of restaurants. Each offering became a revenue center with an associated cost of goods sold for each category. This system felt comfortable and made it easy to have visibility into where we were making or losing money. Each year we have been in business, regardless of the product mix, which has varied greatly, the dollar amount we make as profit when all is said and done, has always been exactly 23 percent. This might sound insignificant, or strange to call attention to, but it's these little winks and nods that make me hear a larger voice, something greater than me saying, "We've got you; you're doing it," that help me to push forward despite my doubts.

As we become who we were meant to be, we slow down, we begin to sit with ourselves in a different way. We begin to know ourselves for who we were truly meant to be versus the identity we constructed to succeed. Finding our "why" is critical for showing up in the world with our best faces forward. It also adds richness and purpose into what can often feel mundane. Starting a business can be repetitive and filled with a lot of "nos." Understanding why you are doing what you are doing, how it benefits others or makes people's lives better, adds richness and can act as a motivating factor, which is key when striking out on your own.

My current work is learning how to be happy where my feet are. When we attach our happiness to our achievements or the things we have collected along the way, we will always come up short. The other sad truth is that reality rarely meets fantasy. If we are always saying, "When this happens, then I will feel ___" (satisfied, happy, fulfilled), then we are setting ourselves up to feel a sense of disappointment once that specific goal is realized.

Being limitless is something I often speak about at Acquire. The power to host events all over the world, not being confined to a space. Being limitless is a part of our culture. Working from anywhere is not only possible, but encouraged. Not having the typical work week schedule is not only possible, but encouraged. This all roots down to building lives that we don't need to escape from. Hard evidence of that is that every year, I take my family on an adventure. Our business model has allowed me to host events from Japan, Albania, and even the slopes of Mt. Etna in Sicily. Our work should bring purpose to lives that are not meant to be grinded away, but meant to be lived.

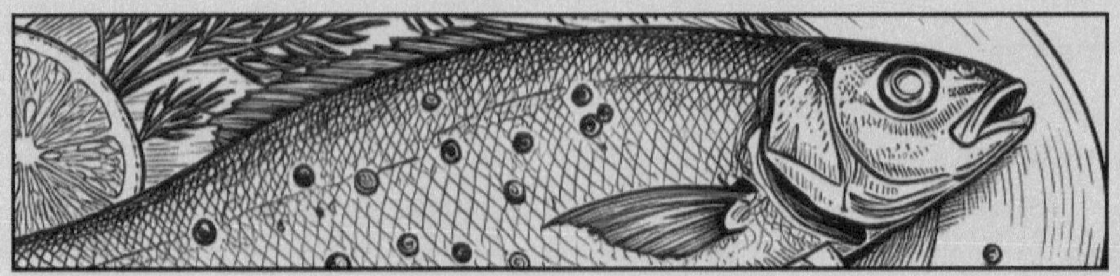

Trout en Brodo with Mushrooms

I have a mild obsession with broth. This broth is light and delicate, a traditional dashi. The mushrooms are lightly pickled to add a touch of acidity, and the fish is crisped with the skin side up. It's light, simple, and nourishing.

Wine Pairing: Trousseau from the Jura

Ingredients
4 trout filets (skin on)
Olive oil
1 lb mixed mushrooms
2 tbsp rice wine vinegar
1 piece of kombu
1 cup bonito flakes

Instructions
1. Sauté mushrooms in olive oil until all the water has evaporated. Place in a bowl off to the side with rice wine vinegar.

2. Fill a stock pot with 4 cups of water and add the kombu. Bring the heat up but don't boil. Allow the kombu to steep like a delicate tea for 30 minutes (or overnight in the fridge).

3. Before it boils, remove the kombu with tongs and add the bonito flakes. Turn off the heat immediately and let it steep for 5 minutes before straining through a fine mesh strainer.

4. If you want to fancy up the broth, steep dried mushrooms and add a touch of mirin for acidity to taste.

5. Salt the fish on both sides and cook in an oiled pan over medium high heat, skin side down, until it is medium in temperature.

6. To serve, add the marinated mushrooms to the bottom of the bowl. Place the cooked fish, skin side up, and pour the broth around.

Chapter 10:

The Endless Reach of the Table

Travel is sacred. Early in my career as a sommelier, I sought out moments of authentic connection with people and places that I had only read about. There was always food, a shared meal. They always made me feel like those old Southern women did: wrapped in a warm blanket. Loved. Wine migrated from a status symbol in my mind to a place where true humanity could be felt and seen and experienced. I have spent my life traveling and utilizing restaurants and shared meals to connect with a culture through the lens of how they dine. Food and wine act as the conduit for breaking language barriers and connecting deeply.

It also is something we, as a family, make a massive priority, meaning there are other things that are sacrificed so that we can take a month every summer and go far and wide. There are never fancy hotels. We carry backpacks and take trains and buses. We cook most of our meals and stay in Airbnbs. I believe that my role as a mother is to show my boys that, despite the devastating news, the world is good. That people, despite having different opinions, values, and belief systems, want to go out of their way to help you and to connect with you.

In 2013, Sean and I backpacked through Vietnam. We took an overnight train from Hanoi to Sa Pa, a remote town in the mountains just forty miles south of the border to China. As we sat on our bunks, a rickety old table that came out from the wall between us, drinking warm Hanoi beer and playing cards, I thought to myself, *Wow, what an adventure*. We knew we wanted kids. In fact, we had been "trying" off and on since before our wedding in

2009. It wasn't time yet, but we didn't know that. Our train pulled in as the sun rose to the most insanely beautiful sight I have ever seen. Rice paddies filled with baby piglets, oxen, ducks, and the most breathtaking mountains. We boarded a local bus up the hill to our hotel, which sat high above the valley. "Trekking" is the only thing on the to-do list in a place like this. We hired a local guide and hiked. Dotted across the landscape were huts with noodles, broth, and low alcohol beer. We would hike about twenty kilometers a day, then return to our hotel and crash. We ran into so many families on the trail, mostly Aussies and Kiwis. I realized then that travel doesn't have to stop once you have children.

As I write this book, my boys are six and eight and have visited fourteen countries despite two years spent in lockdown due to a global pandemic. I am not saying that traveling with kids is easy. I am the last person who will delve into a romanticized false narrative, but this type of travel is wildly rich. It is like all things that you work hard for. Hunter, my oldest, turned four months old in San Sebastièn and ten months old in Kyoto. When my kids were born, I barely broke six figures, which is considered "low income" by Bay Area standards. Even when my salary was $28K a year as a restaurant manager (yes, you read that right), we would save what we could into a travel fund. Travel is important to us, and sharing that with our children became a core principle for our family.

We are often told that retirement is the time to go far and wide. I learned from watching my own parents, who absolutely loved travel, that time is not guaranteed. My father worked in an office for thirty-eight years. He saved and saved and was so smart with the money he earned. Then he got sick. The last ten years of his life, he could barely leave the house. My challenge to you is this: Take that trip, go to that place, experience that thing TODAY because time is not guaranteed, and we shouldn't wait to do the things that light us up.

The following are a collection of writings from trips we've taken over the years, all rooted in connection, hospitality, and rich human experience.

Iceland & Spain, July 2022

As I write this we are sleeping in a trailer on a farm in remote northern Iceland. The family we are staying with are tenth-generation sheep farmers. There are three generations currently living here and five kids under the age of thirteen. They keep asking us why we would come here. It is not a "tourist place." And that is exactly why. There is space here. Real space. My kids get real life experience. Tonight we shared a meal with them: sheep from their farm, around the table. We learned about their history and culture. My kids ran wild with their kids even though they do not share the same language. *This* is why we travel. I had the misconception that travel was going to stop once I had kids, but it only gets richer. Kids are the ultimate connector. They are the most open people on the planet.

As I pick this back up, we have landed in Northern Spain. We've spent this trip living out of two backpacks, moving every two days. We arrived at a small apartment overlooking the sea. We unpacked for the first time. I planted roots. I saw that my family had too, so we amended our trip, giving us a few extra nights. Sticking to "the plan" sometimes doesn't serve everyone. Being open to change means noticing how people are feeling and choosing what is best for *everyone*. As a result of having more time, we spent the day with a winemaking family in their fifth generation. Again, we shared a meal, this time paella, cheese, olives, and cured mussels all paired with the wine they make at their property. Again, we connected around the table with food as the cornerstone. We spoke about wine, of course, and "the business," but we also spoke about raising children, about life during a pandemic, about the Universe and nature and the responsibility our generation has to make real change for the future. Again, our children added to our experience.

We tend to think of adult travel (i.e., Europe) and kid travel (i.e., Disneyland) as separate. Part of having success in merging the two includes slowing down, managing your expectations, letting your kids dictate the pace, and being open to change. Often we put such pressure on our experiences. When the goal is simply to experience the world, and not to accomplish anything, it allows us to be more fully present. It is when the outcome of the journey does not meet the expectation that we are met with disappointment. When we allow whatever is to just "be," we are never disappointed. In fact, we allow ourselves to be more open to the possibility of greatness.

Japan, July 2023

We kicked off a twenty-day backpacking adventure through Japan this week. I have always loved this type of travel. My first real experience traveling the world this way was alone in my early twenties through Europe, with no cell phone, just a *Lonely Planet* guidebook and a one disc CD player with one mixed CD.

When I was younger, I thought that travel like this stopped once you had kids. Don't get me wrong; traveling with small kids isn't easy. They've been all over the world, but it doesn't make them better at traveling. The beautiful thing about kids is that they are exactly how they feel at any given moment. There is a purity to their expression that, when you pause, is refreshing because it's completely unadulterated. That said, it's easy to paint an idyllic picture. This trip has been harder than others. We've stretched these boys further outside their comfort zones than normal.

The most beautiful type of travel, for me, is not comfortable but rich. I believe my job is to show them the world, teach them how to navigate, and show them that, in spite of the news, the world is beautiful and that people are inherently good. It takes work, but it's work I am so grateful to do.

We just left a hostel on the eastern edge of Nagano. We saw snow monkeys in the wild, took night baths in ancient onsen, drank milk and beer on the sidewalk, walked in beautiful forests, traded Pokémon cards, and made new friends from all over the world. Hostels with kids are awesome. People from other countries have that figured out, but we don't. Miles cried when we left.

Now we head to the ocean. We're going to root down for a bit in a couple of days. We've been at it nine days and are almost to the halfway point. We move between overjoyed, to spicy, to emo in a matter or moments.

We've spent the last five days by the ocean. This location is pretty remote. We took a bus eighty-four stops, to a train, to another bus to get here. We've met a few Europeans but no Americans except one sweet Japanese-American family that owns a hotel up the road. They travel the world and homeschool their six kids. They spend a few months a year here in Shimoda to operate the hotel. Immediately, our kids were connected by Pokémon and running circles around their bar. We left the hotel last night and walked out to the beach. A Japanese family was set up lighting off fireworks. They immediately handed our kids sparklers and included us in their fun despite the clear language barrier.

Kids are the ultimate connectors. Traveling with them is tough at times, but they open up parts of the world that may have been inaccessible otherwise. There is a lot about traveling like this with small people that is hard. I won't sugarcoat that, but they slow you down. They open new connections. They see the world with such purity.

Unreasonable Hospitality, July 2024

There is an ancient code of honor called Besa—translating to the kind of hospitality that can restore one's faith in humanity.
—Exploring Albania, Europe's Hidden Gem in the Balkans
(Condé Nast)

Will Guidara, one of my favorite restaurateurs, wrote a book called *Unreasonable Hospitality,* in which he describes his journey taking Eleven Madison Park from mediocre to the number one restaurant in the world by deploying his variations on hospitality. Guidara believes there's nobility in service. He believes that unreasonable hospitality involves creating extraordinary experiences by giving people more than they expect while being absolutely unreasonable in your quest to take care of others. We believe in that too.

We just wrapped a couple of days in Corfu and a week in Albania. I see unreasonable hospitality everywhere when I travel.

Maybe it's because there is vulnerability in being in a foreign place; maybe it's because everything that seems beautiful is even more exaggerated when far from home. Our first day in Corfu was my forty-second birthday. We took a taxi to a far-away beach, and when we went to pay, the driver asked for cash only, which we did not have.

"No problem!" she said, "I will bring you home later. You can pay me then. What time shall I be here?"

Unreasonable hospitality. The next day she drove us to the ferry, stopping first at the ticket station to let me buy tickets on my own with no bags or kids and then took us all the way into the terminal. Unreasonable hospitality. Unreasonable hospitality is everywhere if you choose to see the world that way. The shopkeeper at the store below our apartment in Albania playfully teasing my kids is another example. Every day they'd run down to greet him. He became their friend even though they didn't share the same language. The hotel worker who threw my kids in the air in the pool for more than an hour and promptly high-fived them when we returned the next day. The woman who gave me her phone to use as a hotspot so I could take an important work call when service was failing me. The sweet people at the farmers' market who fed me cheese, oil, fruit, and even brandy at 10 a.m. because they didn't have the language to explain to me what I was looking at. All unreasonable hospitality.

I believe that hospitality is a mindset. It is a way to choose to move in the world. It is being open. It is choosing to make eye contact and say hello to strangers. It is being loving with your actions and your mannerisms even when a common language is not shared. It is choosing to go out of your way for others for no other reason than because you care about how you make people feel.

Japan, Summer 2025

This is the time of year that I pack up my family and venture into the world. Part of anchoring a business to virtual events means flexibility and freedom, which means we can host events literally anytime, anywhere. We are hosting several events while on the road spanning nine time zones and two continents. Designing a life we don't have to escape from is a core tenet at Acquire.

This summer, we head back to Japan. Japan is a place we return to again and again. It is a thoughtful culture that is rooted in hospitality and composed of people dedicated to their craft. There is an intentionality to the culture that makes the lives of the people that live there better. This will be my nine-year-old's third visit, which I am humbly aware is a bit ridiculous. This July, we will be on the northern island of Hokkaido, which, true to form, is off the beaten path. Part of venturing out into the lesser-traveled parts of the world is about discovering the soul of the people who live there. Big cities tend to be busy and international and often lacking the traditional elements that you discover when you venture out into the country. Regardless of location, I find that getting out of the city can be like stepping back in time. The path less taken has been a bit of a theme in my life, which I trace back to my early travel days post culinary school in Europe. I spent about six months using the little money I made bartending at night to fund my solo excursions. It was just me and my *Lonely Planet* guidebook, not a cell phone in sight. I learned early on that I would gladly sacrifice things for experiences. It is probably no coincidence that I have found my purpose crafting intimate experiences for others.

Our trip is about a month long. Balancing working remotely with full-time parenting plus international travel is no small feat, but it is always worth it. To add even more complexity, this is the first trip I have taken with my kids where we have some free days, meaning we don't know where we are going to stay. I did this intentionally to breathe space into our experience, to allow for things to unfold as they will, and to open us up to new adventures. When your kids are small, you have to have every minute of international travel planned because, well, parenting small kids is hard enough without dragging them halfway across the world. My boys are seven and nine now, so teaching them how to be open to the world while being flexible and adaptable is intentional. I find that this transfers into how we live our lives back at home as well. Travel is the best education for people of all ages.

We will return first to Kamakura, which is a town south of Tokyo that feels like San Diego-meets-Berkeley-meets-Japan and is loaded with slow-food restaurants. We will visit the Nikka distillery, which was founded in Yiochi in 1934. We will also see a few wine producers, a couple of which are owned by our friends in Burgundy. I am a firm believer that food and drink are connectors of people regardless of location. Japan is certainly no exception.

The Japanese Ikigai, July 2025

"Iki" means life while "gai" means worth or value. The concept of ikigai is not about having a grand purpose, rather finding meaning in the mundane, in the everyday. Ikigai is found at the intersection of what brings you joy, what you are good at, what the world needs, and finally what you can be paid for. It is believed that when you find your ikigai, you have the potential to live a longer life that is more fulfilled. Ikigai is not just about what you do for a living. It goes beyond that. It is believed that our motivation is proportionally tied to how much we care about something. The culture here in Japan is a culture that deeply cares about everything really.

Over the weekend, we returned to one of our favorite restaurants in Kamakura: Beau Temps. The owner, Roy, was the only person working. He was the chef, waiter, sommelier, and maître'd. This restaurant was his grandfather's summer home, which he converted into an intimate space that serves a two-course lunch and dinner menu. He serves only natural wine, meaning wine made from the land with respect for nature, as naturally as possible. This also isn't his primary job. He lived in the US for some time, and got his master's degree in marketing from Northwestern. Today, he is a professor at the university in Kamakura. When I asked him why he would open a restaurant, he responded, "I love wine." He direct-imports a few producers himself. He is also a jazz pianist who gigs a few times a month. He put on a few tunes, which Sean loved. Sean majored in jazz composition and plays nearly every instrument under the sun, so he and Roy had an immediate unspoken bond. You can see by the way that he smiles with his eyes that Roy has clearly found his ikigai.

I have come to believe over the years that my greater purpose is connecting people in a deep and meaningful way. I came to this purpose through the lens of food and wine, but the greater purpose feels richer, deeper somehow. I can honestly say that I never thought that our primary medium for connection would be virtual events. I had never even used Zoom prior to 2020, but it is a powerful tool when used the right way. On our first early morning in Tokyo, we hosted a virtual event for thirty guests across the US. Our event host was in Portugal, I was in Tokyo, and my team was in California and Brooklyn. On our pre-call alone we had three continents and four time zones represented. The power to bring people together across multiple locations has never been easier. What feels more important to me personally is making these engagements mean something, leaving an impression that makes the shared experience stand out. Real connection is felt, not experienced. Being with Roy, in that beautiful little space, I *felt* connection. The juxtaposition, I suppose, is that while I have traveled halfway across the world to get that feeling, what I do professionally doesn't require a plane ticket, a hotel, or an overnight, just a computer and a willingness to be open-minded to the power of connection that can be found in the virtual space.

The Japanese Omotenashi, July 2025

Omotenashi is a Japanese concept encompassing a unique and selfless approach to hospitality. It runs deeper than just providing a service. It is rooted in anticipating needs with meticulous attention to detail without expecting anything in return. I often preach about hospitality as a "way of being." The Japanese omotenashi is just that. Japan has a service culture where every detail is created with how someone will experience it in mind. On my first trip here, I was blown away by the thoughtful attention to detail. In every restroom stall, there was even a high chair type seat where I could put my baby. The subways in Tokyo each pipe in different sounds of nature or classical music. Every station is different. The intention is to add some calm to commuters' everyday travel. It is done for no other reason than to make people's day better. The other day, I stumbled upon an honor bar "things store" that was created just to spark joy, that feeling you get when you stumble upon a treasure, or find something that feels like it was meant for you.

Gift-giving is also a large part of the culture here. I was at the grocery store with my oldest son, and an older Japanese woman came up to him and gave him a token for the dry ice machine. It is very hot here, so when you bag your groceries you have a few choices to make as far as cooling systems go for your transport home. She took his hand and opened it, placed the coin in his palm while smiling, bowing, and exuding joy from her eyes. She then reached into her bag and pulled out some peaches in syrup and handed it to him, bowing and smiling. We bowed and thanked her repeatedly. The richest form of human connection can be found anywhere anytime, no foreign language skills required.

My hospitality background makes me immediately reference "surprise and delight," which is a tactic we often incorporate as an additional touch, a way of saying, "I thought of you, so here is something I thought you would like." Even the local pharmacist found gifts for our boys. Making people feel seen and appreciated is a core tenant of hospitality and omotenashi. Japan is a place I love to return to because the culture is rooted in hospitality. Being hospitality-centered is all about doing things for others for no other reason than you care about how you make people *feel.*

* * *

This most recent trip to Hokkaido was filled with so many incredibly rich moments. There was one moment, in particular, we were staying in a cabin on a beautiful remote lake called Lake Toya. There wasn't much of anything out there, so every day our activity consisted of walking down to the lake for a swim. I was sitting on the beach watching my boys and Sean swim out in the distance, and I was overcome with a sense of peace and gratitude.

Thank god we fought for this, echoed loudly in my mind. So often, when we are faced with the hardest things, our instincts say to run, to protect ourselves from further pain. Running, in many cases, is far easier than sitting with the discomfort, than working through the things that are really really difficult. Building a life you don't need to escape from requires discomfort. It is often an incredibly slow process. It is not for the faint of heart and rarely do you get a big "ah ha" moment that tells you you're on the right path. Consistency is paramount.

German Chocolate Cake

My mom made this cake for my dad's birthday for forty-eight consecutive years. It was his absolute favorite dessert on earth. This is fitting as the upcoming chapter details his death day, his sacred and beautiful departure from this earth.

Wine Pairing: Bual or Malmsey Madeira

Ingredients

1 cup unsalted butter
2 cups sugar
4 egg yolks
¼ lb German sweet chocolate
½ cup boiling water
2 ½ cups all purpose flour
1 cup buttermilk
1 tsp baking soda
1 tsp vanilla extract
pinch of salt
4 stiffly beaten egg whites

Icing
1 cup sugar
1 cup evaporated milk
1 stick butter
3 beaten egg yolks
2 cups flaked coconut
1 tsp vanilla extract
1 cup chopped pecans

Instructions

1. Cream together the butter and sugar. Add the egg yolks one at a time.

2. Melt the chocolate in boiling water and add it to the mixture

3. Add flour alternately with buttermilk after dissolving the baking soda into the buttermilk.

4. Add vanilla extract and salt and fold in stiffly beaten egg whites.

5. Bake in three 9-inch cake pans for 30 minutes at 350 degrees.

6. Cook sugar, evaporated milk, butter, and egg yolks together in a double boiler, stirring constantly. Add coconut, vanilla, and nuts and spread mixture between layers and on the top of the cake.

CHAPTER 11

When Gathering Meets Goodbye

Bearing the unbearable is the deepest root of compassion in the world. When you bear what you think you can not bear, who you think you are dies. You become the compassion. You don't have compassion; you are compassion. True compassion goes beyond empathy to being with the experience of another. You become an instrument of compassion.
—Ram Dass

If service in restaurants is like a gateway drug, caretaking an ailing family member is like heroin. My father's death was an otherworldly experience that changed me at my core by teaching me how I want to move in this world.

My father continued to decline in health over the years but always bounced back. A series of strokes and TIAs made his speech slurred. A brain aneurysm in 2018 put him in a wheelchair for good. I compared that episode to a hamster I had as a kid that died and came back to life. We had an admittedly morbid relationship with his mortality. Thankfully, he found it hilarious. He got to the point where he couldn't do much of anything for himself. He was fed and bathed by my mother and a handful of caregivers who became like family. We used a crane-like tool to get him in and out of bed. He was still joyful though. He loved my boys. We live two miles away from the house I grew up in, so he had a front-row seat to their craziness at least two days a week. He would get uncontrollable giggles when they were around. That joy was infectious. It made my life richer.

In the midst of Acquire's greatest transformation to date, I had the great honor of my life—caring for my dad during the last days of his life. The reality is that as we are building all of these things, life is still happening, and oftentimes life can be breathtakingly beautiful. Regardless of what God you might pray to, I believe that giving ourselves over to the service of others in this deeply intimate way puts us closer to the Divine.

Artist Jason Reynolds describes caretaking for his mother as prayer: "It is praying at the only creator I have ever actually known. What else could prayer be? Prayer can't just be asking for things."

To me, prayer is anything sacred. It is being in the space of pure love. It is caring for someone deeply. It is going out of your way for others. It is the purest and deepest form of love.

We spent my dad's final week in a cocoon of sorts. There was love and purity balanced by anticipation of grief. It reminded me of the hibernation phase after giving birth. The similarities are not lost on me. We leave this world in the same state we arrive—helpless and completely dependent upon the people who love us. There was food and wine and music and friends. His deathbed became a table, a gathering place that was filled with so much love. I filled the room with photos of family and friends and the flowers he loved. I rubbed oils on him, burned sage and palo santo, and we surrounded him with all of the people he loved most in the world. People came by to see him, to pray over him. My boys were there, drawing pictures and playing on the floor by his bed. Having my children there to bear witness was filled with countless lessons I could never have taught them. There is so much power in vulnerability, in allowing your heart to break open in front of the people you love only to show them how resilient you are. Our society has a wildly fractured relationship with death. Turns out, easing a life out of this world can be as miraculous and beautiful as bringing life into it.

Our final night with him, probably not coincidentally, also involved a restaurant: Bellotti, his favorite. We ordered in and ate off of paper plates while sitting on the bed with him. We drank his favorite wine, a bottle of Vosne-Romanée. Although he could not eat or drink, the mood was celebratory. I played a lot of Paul Simon while he was transitioning, which was a shared favorite. I even asked him to send me Paul Simon songs when he got wherever he was going so I would know he was okay, that he made it. Once it became clear that we only had a few moments left with him, we were quiet. As he drew his last breath, it was peaceful, like air slowly leaking out of a balloon, then stopped. I put my head on his chest and heard his heart stop beating, and I grabbed a bottle of Champagne. We toasted him and cried. I heard a song playing low on the stereo. It was Paul Simon's "Gone At Last," one I had never heard before but with remarkable timing. This song is joyful. It is about redemption, freedom, and release from suffering. The next song that came on was "Another One Bites the Dust,' and we all laughed through our tears, assuming that if he was somehow controlling the stereo, he was certainly trying to lighten the mood. "Rocket Man" came on next, and we cranked up the volume on his favorite sound system, all belting at the top of our lungs, tears streaming down our faces. I looked across the bed and saw his baby brother, whom he absolutely adored, singing and crying, and my heart burst open into a million pieces.

This, I thought, *this is love.*

The body without a soul is a wild thing. When they took him, I wasn't ready. I just sat in that room for hours after he was gone, thinking, *What now? What are we all going to do now?* Helping him die only took a matter of days, but it was all-consuming. I was with him alone at the hospital earlier that week when we decided to stop treating him. I held his hand while they pulled out the tubes and wires and the ambulance came to take him home. Walking *out* of the hospital, a place where I logged so many hours with him, over half of my life, knowing that we wouldn't be back there together was an insane feeling. All of the doctors and nurses stood to the sides of the hallways with compassion in their eyes, a softness that conveyed a million words, mostly of shared heartache and love. I promised him I would be there until the very end, and that meant the icky parts too. Being an only child is a trip when things like this happen. Once his body was gone, I just sat in the room we created for him, that sacred space. I felt like it was the closest I would ever be again to his essence, like the only remaining parts of him would seep out the walls, and I needed to soak it up while I still could.

I now know that our loved ones don't go far when they go. In those early days, I felt my dad's presence everywhere. There were blatant signs and clear communication. Those have tapered off in the year since his passing, but I am convinced now that the veil of human experience is thin, that what we perceive is only a small glimpse of the magnitude of what *is*.

My love, I was so wrong. Dying is the opposite of leaving. When I left my body, I did not go away. That portal of light was not a portal to elsewhere, but a portal to right here. I am more here than I ever was before. So close you look past me when wondering where I am. It's OK. I know that to be human is to be farsighted. But feel me now, walking the chambers of your heart, pressing my palms into the soft walls of your living. Why did no one tell us to die is to be reincarnated in those we love while they are still alive? Ask me the altitude of heaven, and I will answer: "How tall are you?"
—Andrea Gibson

I've long wrapped my sadness in gratitude for the gift of additional time, but the reality is that what made my dad left his physical body long before I felt the weight of his soul leave the room on that beautiful night in November. Grief is not just missing the person that is gone but all of the things that came before, all of the micro losses you experience when you watch your person disappear before your eyes.

We often suffer because we are so attached to the outcomes we want, not the outcomes that are clearly in front of us. We hold on to wanting this person to stay when they need to go. If the intention of modern medicine is to keep people alive, then the common and incorrect perception is that when they die, it's a failure. But it's not. It is one of the most beautiful transformations I have ever had the privilege of bearing witness to.

As I ironed my boys' shirts in my kitchen for my dad's funeral it dawned on me: Rites of passage come in all shapes and sizes. Often rites of passage are celebrated milestones: buying a home, having a baby. But losing a parent is a rite of passage as well. I learned some major life lessons through stewarding this wild transition, mostly reinforcing that the suffering comes from what we cling to the most. We are often taught to separate personal life from work, that certain things aren't appropriate. It can be incredibly powerful when you allow your biggest life moments to inform your professional life. It gives us profound empathy for others, offering a deeper lens to connect with grace and understanding to those around us.

The world changed the day my dad left it. It doesn't matter how subtle the shift; we all leave an imprint, a mark on the world and a void when we go that creates a ripple effect. There is an unexpected openness and ease. The realization that your body is always on high alert when you are in and out of emergencies and hospitals. My shoulders have come down. The way I approach my business and how I run it has found an unexpected place of equanimity, mostly rooted in the knowing that nothing is life or death, but death itself. Once you know that truth in your bones, being less attached to outcomes becomes far easier.

When the elemental people in our lives go, we often get caught in the loop of grief. We remember the good times, the not-so-good times and everything in between. Initially, I had a hard time figuring out where I ended and he began. His force was so strong. What we forget to notice is that change in the world that happens when they go can also kick off a jolt of inspiration, of creation. When we reached the one year anniversary of his death, I was mesmerized by what had transpired. I wrote this book. I built my business into what I was dreaming of a year ago. I am building a sales funnel for the Michelin restaurant group that hired me long, long ago after having an idea that planted a seed that has grown into a partnership. Of course, those things have been work, but the creation came from making space. Not just physical space, but mental space, opening up parts of myself to allow the flow of creativity to happen where it may have once been stifled. I miss him terribly. I guess I always will, but I am also tremendously grateful for all of the gifts he gave me and continues to give me despite his physical absence.

Something about this experience made me realize that all of these things we are chasing, we can't take any of it with us. In the end, there is only pure love. It also helped me to fully release to what is, and in doing so, a path unfolded before me that was exactly where I was trying to go. Only this time, for the first time, it felt effortless.

There can be tremendous suffering in the grasping, in trying to become some*body* or some*thing*. Letting go and shedding identity is also a death of sorts. It is often painful. It shakes you at your core, but there is so much beauty and power to be found in the surrender, in the letting go, the removing of what "should" to what "is."

You have to become somebody before becoming nobody. When you become nobody, there is no tension, no pretense, no one trying to be anyone or anything. The natural state of the mind shines through unobstructed, and the natural state of the mind is pure love.
—Ram Dass

David Brooks eloquently describes the concept of *The Second Mountain* in his 2019 book by that name. He says that everyone has two lives: the one you are told to want and the one you quietly crave. On your first mountain, you establish an identity separate from your parents, build a secure ego, and try to make your mark on the world, mostly through the lens of external success. Then something life-altering happens that sends you tumbling down into the valley. It is only in this valley of despair that you can finally make out your second mountain. It is in that valley where you discover your most powerful yearnings. So you don't climb the second mountain the way you climbed the first. You surrender to it. The first mountain is all about ambition, acquisition, and independence. You are conquered by your second mountain. You can spot the people on their second mountain out in the wild. They're often entrepreneurs, community leaders, and explorers following heart-centered missions toward greater authenticity.

Success, to me, is being happy where my feet are. It is picking my children up from school, taking walks among the trees, and having meandering conversations. It is being able to truly be there, in all the mundane parts of their lives and the lives of others that I hold sacred. It is making space to be quiet in my day, to feel thankful for the gift of this life. To be curious about what I create and the impact it might have on others. It is being hopeful that my words and actions throughout each day impact others in a positive and uplifting way. Often, when I compare myself to others, I try to feel into what their day to day would feel like. Maybe they're always doing glamorous things, or traveling the world, or drinking crazy wine, and more often than not, I feel relieved to be right where I am. Not because I have it figured out, far from it. Not because I am living my dream life. That is still a work in progress. But because the life we create for ourselves is a reflection of us at any given moment in time. It's okay to just be yourself, right where you are, perfectly imperfect.

The truth is we are always becoming. There are countless versions of us that show up at the table: the new mother, the sommelier, the friend, the business owner. There are empty seats as well, seats that hold space for who we are yet to become, set beautifully, a gift to our future selves. To age is the ultimate gift. I look forward to meeting those future versions of myself, rooted in authenticity, wrapped in rich community, held in real human connection and grace.

Grandma Adah's Coconut Oatmeal Cookies

This is my paternal grandmother's recipe. Adah Guild had a master's degree in home economics. She was from Oklahoma and was a brilliant homemaker who stayed home to raise her three boys.

Ingredients

¾ cup butter

2 cups light brown sugar

1 ½ cups all purpose flour

½ tsp salt

1 tsp vanilla extract

1 tsp baking soda

3 cups quick oats

1 cup coconut flakes

Pecans, raisins, or chocolate chips as desired

Instructions

1. Beat the room temperature butter and brown sugar until fluffy.

2. Add the other ingredients until well combined.

3. Bake at 350 degrees until lightly browned (about 12-14 minutes).

What I Wish Every Restaurateur Knew About the Business of Bringing People to The Table

As I was writing this book, I kept feeling the tug to share some more practical, how-to types of insights I have gained in my journey. So this section was created for restaurateurs. I have spent countless hours thinking through how my experience in growing a business outside of a brick and mortar could translate to the hospitality space. Restaurants are maybe the only business in the world with no outbound sales function. We discuss how to sell once the guests are sitting at the table, but we spend little to no time talking through how to get them to the table in the first place. Imagine being in the tech industry, creating a piece of software that you pour your heart, soul, and entire wallet into, and then just waiting for someone to come buy it. People would think you were crazy; yet, in restaurants, that is exactly what we do. We lean into public relations (PR), which is not a substitution for lead-generating marketing. The hospitality space needs to realize:

No one is coming to save you.

That truth can feel insurmountable. A common thread that unites the best and the brightest in the restaurant world is resilience, a commitment to foraging a pathway forward even when the problem feels too big, too scary, too real. So here I share the "extra ingredients" I believe, and have been working

with restaurateurs in implementing, in order to bring guests to
our tables.

It is commonplace to hear CEOs talk about how they utilize the
transferable skills they learned waiting tables in college to run their
organization. Rarely do we hear it the other way around. Turns
out, the skills acquired (pun intended) when building a business
that serves the corporate world offer incredible insight into how
other industries sell their products and services. It might be hard
to believe, but even the most savvy restaurateurs aren't utilizing
these strategies. My purpose is not to nitpick the industry that
I love with all of my heart but rather to highlight a pathway for
restaurateurs to take their power back. Restaurants are desperate
for consistent revenue.

> **If we applied the same go-to-market strategy to
> the hospitality space that is utilized by the rest of
> the sales world, could we save restaurants?**

So What Is a Sales Strategy?

In any industry where you have something to sell, there are
inbound and outbound sales. All restaurants field inbound sales
by taking reservations. They also take requests for private dining,
which often take far too long to reply to, and many restaurants miss
countless dollars in opportunities, but I will leave that for another
soapbox. However, there usually is no clear strategy for outbound,
meaning targeting specific customer types based upon your sales
history and going after them in an aim to turn them into customers.

There is also a systemic problem that must be shifted that starts
at the top. The culture in restaurants runs *deep*. It is my favorite
thing about the restaurant business. That said, the new guard wants
to be developed. They crave balance. They demand inclusion. They
require opportunities for growth. They speak up for themselves
where we did not. As a subset, we can be pretty married to the
"way we do things," which does not leave space for change. Our
community is rife for transformation, desperate for it. The first step

is a shift in mindset, which requires the ability to break down what we know with a willingness to consider putting it back together in a different way. So how do we start?

Retool How You Define "High Value" Work

Restaurants put their most valuable people in the wrong positions. In an *all hands on deck* environment, where guest experience reigns supreme and hustle culture is not only glorified but also expected in order for the machine to run, there is no rank or title that opts you out of service. Rather than hiring a director of events and marketing, hire a real marketer, someone who, dare I say, *can't work service. (*audible gasp*)*

Why?! Because ...

**If your sales person is pouring water,
they aren't driving revenue.**

Someone with a background in building a go-to-market strategy will understand how to target your ideal customers using specific, calculated, and automated tools. They will focus their full efforts on driving revenue for your business. The quick response I anticipate from restaurateurs is: "I can't afford that." Revenue driving positions are always worth the spend. Yes, there will be an initial investment, but eventually this position will pay for itself in dividends.

IG Is Sexy, but Your Customers Are on LinkedIn

I get it: Everyone wants to be an influencer. Also, that food shot got a lot of likes. When it comes to business-to-business (B2B) marketing, 82 percent of B2B marketers have seen the greatest success with LinkedIn, while 84 percent of restaurants are on Meta. Corporate clients drive private event revenue, which is a restaurant's most controllable sale based upon predetermined menus, product cost, and labor. If you want customers with a healthy budget, you must target corporate diners. Look at the titles and companies of people who have hosted buyouts in the past, retool your dining room to maximize event space, and make private event revenue your focus. This is the quickest pathway to controllable, predictable, and dependable revenue. Everything else becomes icing on the cake. And you can still have the secret menu that Gen Z will photograph when they come in and don't drink.

PR Is Not a Sales Strategy

Everyone wants to be the next Mario Batali! Oh wait, not him, but you get the idea. Having a publicist is important to maintain the messaging and image once you're nearing the top of the food chain, but for everyone else, which let's be honest, is most of us, driving revenue utilizing a calculated sales strategy comes before PR. A common pitfall is that restaurateurs substitute PR for marketing and sales, assuming they will achieve the same metrics. Neither are a substitute for a strategic sales strategy.

TERMS TO KNOW

SALES FUNNEL

Building a sales funnel is about connecting to the people who need your services often before they are ready to buy. By targeting and retargeting a select group that fit your customer profile through email marketing, social media and ads, you put your brand top of mind so that when the need arises, they come to you first.

CUSTOMER RELATIONSHIP MANAGEMENT

CRM is a tool that is used for managing conversations with current and potential customers. CRMs give you automation, which means that emails are going out while you're doing something else, a crucial tool in the hospitality industry, where time is of the essence.

IDEAL CUSTOMER PROFILE

What are the common qualities and characteristics of your ideal customers? Get super clear and detailed about your ICP, including identifying who has the budget, who makes the decisions, who has a need that your product fills? Targeting your ICPs directly shortens the time to make the sale. Keep in mind that people who plan events in your area may or may not live there, so for large scale outreach purposes, we are not as tied to a specific geographic location.

OUTBOUND CAMPAIGNS

Campaigns are how you communicate with your ICP. Email, LinkedIn, social media, phone calls. The campaigns are simply a series of steps linked together with the intention of turning a prospect into a customer over time.

IDEAL CUSTOMER

Once you have identified your ICP, here is how to expand your connection with them …

GET YOUR ICP TO FOLLOW YOU ON LI

Use an automated tool to increase your LI following w/ ICPs. There are tools, like Skylead, that integrate with Sales Navigator. You can drop your ICP list from Sales Navigator into this tool, and it can do automated outreach to follow and connect with (and send messages to) your ideal customers.

GET MORE CLARITY ON WHO TO TARGET

Look at all of your past private event clients and look for consistencies. There are tech tools that can scan these lists for you. Try Clay, which can also pull out your past guests' job titles, company names, phone, and email information.

FIND LOOK ALIKES

Use LI Sales Navigator search function to pull out more people that look like your target ICP. What job titles do they have? What size companies do they work for? What other companies are in close proximity to your restaurant?

Bringing people to the table requires a targeted approach, a strategy. By utilizing this proactive approach, and being targeted in your outreach, you will begin to see a return on your efforts to connect with new guests. There is an investment of time and likely money to make this happen, but the smartest investments we make in any business are those directly tied to revenue generation. Restaurants are too important to fail. By taking a step back and creating something entirely new, I gained a lens into the hospitality space that I believe can be wildly beneficial. The goal, as always, is to help people. I love restaurants with all of my heart. My hope is that by implementing these tools, you can ease some of the burden associated with an inability to drive revenue.

Bonus Ingredients

CREATE A LI SOCIAL MEDIA STRATEGY

Who will be the voice of your restaurant? What can they say that your ICP will be interested in hearing about?

SEO

Work with a marketer to optimize your SEO by selecting keywords that your ICP might use to find you. You can direct prospective clients to your website and then use tools like Instantly to capture their information so you can retarget them with an additional touchpoint like an email or phone call.

SET UP YOUR CRM

There are many free or inexpensive tools that integrate to Sales Navigator. You will build cadences with your messaging that will include email and LI messages to your target list.

CREATE OUTBOUND CAMPAIGNS

What are you trying to sell? What do you want people to hear? The campaigns will need to have several touchpoints and will need to feel as personal as possible.

REPORTING

Measure your success by how many email opens you are getting, how many replies, and the click rate. Take people who are consistently opening your messages and put them into a new campaign.

ADS

While sometimes unnecessary, advertising on LI can be very effective because you have the ability to target the folks who are in your current campaigns and fit your ICP.

HIRING

Hire a real marketer who can run social media plus email marketing, ads, and outbound marketing. This person will be the voice of your business. They will likely come from a field outside of restaurants. A good marketer doesn't need to have worked in the restaurant industry to understand how to market to those who need restaurants. This could even be a gig worker or part-time contractor (versus the financial burden of a $250K yearly salary) to help drive the growth needed. The benefit should greatly outweigh the cost.

CENTRALIZE THE SYSTEM

Centralizing your sales team is great if you are able, meaning getting them out of the restaurant so that they can respond to guests quickly and efficiently, which is key for conversion. According to a survey by WorkPulse, 70 percent of guests will go elsewhere after a delayed response over twenty-four hours, especially for high-value group or private dining bookings where planning is urgent and options are plentiful. In fact, the conversion rate for inquiries drops from 20 percent within one hour to around 5 percent within twenty-four hours, and then to an estimated 2 percent or lower after twenty-four hours. A hungry sales person will not only go after new leads, but also increase conversion rates just by being available when other restaurants are not.

Acknowledgments

To my boys, all three of you, thank you for being my North Star, for bringing so much light into my life. I am so grateful for our unit of four. Oftentimes I look at the three of you, and I can't even believe you're mine. I look forward to the adventures we will go on and the memories we will create together. Home is truly wherever you three are.

Sean, thank you for walking through this life with me. Thank you for inspiring me to do better, to be better and for all of your wisdom and guidance. You are a sage that I am so grateful to have in my corner.

To my babies, I have fallen in love with every single version of you. I don't long for the chubby babies of the past, but relish in the who-you-are-now. Being your Mama is the absolute greatest gift of my life. Hunter, my quiet observer and deep empath. You, my love, are my greatest teacher. Miles, my barnacle baby, your love is so rich. To be loved by you is life's greatest gift.

To my Mom, who has shown by example what true dedication means. You've been the glue, my entire life, that has held this mess together. Thank you for your unconditional support and love. Thank you for loving Dad like you did and for giving him the end of life he truly deserved. You are deserving of endless love and good fortune. I am so grateful for you.

To everyone who has helped me build Acquire, thank you for your devotion and contribution. Whether our time together was years long or brief, know that you left a mark. I have learned so much from each of you. Your impact is immeasurable.

To my Moon Circle Mamas. Thank you for community, for allowing me to show up in my true authenticity. For reading this thing when it was so, so rough and for holding space for all of my feelings as it moved into the world.

Bulla, my sister-friend, thank you for being there through it all and always showing up when I need you most.

Finally, to the ladies at Synergy Publishing Group, just wow. Thank you for creating a community of like-minded (mostly) women to write with. Showing up, on Zoom, and connecting deeply as we all poured our hearts out on paper was so incredibly powerful. Women in community is where it's *at*.

About the Author

Haley Moore is a connector and a creative who finds joy in bringing people together for authentic, meaningful experiences. As a mother, entrepreneur, and lifelong learner, she believes that moments shared around the table—and in community—hold the power to heal and inspire.

Though Haley's path includes recognition as a nationally acclaimed sommelier, wine educator and founder of Acquire, these achievements are only one part of her story. What defines her most is her devotion to presence, generosity, and helping others feel truly seen and connected—the table acting as the sacred space where food and wine become the connective tissue for building authentic community.